# OPERATORS AND THINGS

# OPERATORS AND THINGS

## The Inner Life of a Schizophrenic

### BARBARA O'BRIEN

Foreword by Melanie Villines
Introduction by Michael Maccoby, Ph.D.
Afterword by Colleen Delegan

Featuring photographs from the Library of Congress collection

SILVER BIRCH PRESS
LOS ANGELES, CALIFORNIA

Foreword & Conversation with Michael Maccoby ©2011, Melanie Villines

Afterword ©2011, Colleen Delegan

*Operators and Things*, originally published by Arlington Books, 1958

2011 edition, ©2011 Silver Birch Press

**ISBN-13:** 978-0615509280

**ISBN-10:** 0615509282

Photographs by Esther Bubley, Russell Lee, and John Vachon from the Library of Congress collection

**Cover photo:** *Passengers standing in aisles on Memphis-Chattanooga Greyhound bus, 1943, by Esther Bubley*

**Email:** silver@silverbirchpress.com
**Web:** silverbirchpress.com
**Blog:** silverbirchpress.wordpress.com

**Mailing Address:**
Silver Birch Press
P.O. Box 29458
Los Angeles, CA 90029
USA

# Contents

# Foreword

My experience with *Operators and Things* began about thirty years ago, when I discovered a hardcover copy for twenty-five cents at a yard sale. At the time, I was partial to sci-fi novels by Philip K. Dick and the shamanic tales of Carlos Castaneda – and Barbara O'Brien's book seemed to fit right in with the work of these otherworldly writers.

I found *Operators and Things* nearly impossible to put down – it was a true story, but read like a thriller. As I raced through the pages, I was awed by the author's compelling style and distinctive voice. This was *some* story – and s*ome* writer.

As soon as I finished the book, I wrote to Barbara in care of her publisher to gain permission to adapt *Operators and Things* into a play. During the late 1970s and early 1980s, I was active in the Chicago theater scene – as an actor, playwright, and director – and helped found a theater company, where I workshopped more than a dozen of my plays. My letter to Barbara was returned because the publisher had ceased operations. I asked my sister, a librarian, to do some research and she uncovered several other firms that had released editions of the book. I wrote to Barbara in care of these publishers, but received no reply. Through the copyright office, I obtained the name of Barbara's agent and sent a letter to his New York office – but discovered he had retired. Subsequently, I learned that the agent had published several memoirs in which he'd referenced his involvement with *Operators and Things*.

From the agent's writings, I understood that Barbara had written the book as a form of therapy. She picked the agent's name at random from Literary Market Place, and sent him the manuscript. He immediately recognized the book's value and tried to place it with over a dozen publishers before a friend at a small press bought the rights. *Operators and Things* was later resold to an even smaller press, which issued the book as its first offering.

In 2010, I exchanged email messages with the original publisher, a man who has gone on to become an esteemed diplomat, foreign policy consultant, and historian. In response to my questions about the origins of *Operators and Things*, he replied: "Two friends of mine and I started a short-lived publishing company back in the 1950s. We bought a number of titles from another publishing company that was downsizing; among them was *Operators and Things*."

Even though it was a startup operation, the publisher did an outstanding job getting the word out about *Operators and Things*. The book was widely reviewed and written about and, for the most part, given high praise. Reviewers described the book as "remarkable," "extraordinary," "astonishing," and "brilliant." In *National Review*, William F. Buckley wrote, "...with penetration and satisfying imagery, Miss O'Brien (a pseudonym) describes her psychosis, from which unaccountably and spontaneously she recovers."

The book was accepted by opinion leaders in the psychiatric mainstream, as evidenced by a 1959 review in the *Archives of General Psychiatry*. The review read, in part, "A report on schizophrenia as seen from that usually inaccessible point of observation, the patient, cannot but be welcomed by the student of this disorder and by the psychiatrist who must deal with it. This small book...brings into high focus some of the ever-intriguing problems of schizophrenia. The trained investigator will recognize them. Yet in writing down her experiences as a patient, the author is contributing irreplaceably to our knowledge. It may be said at the outset that any person in the field can read the book with profit and enjoyment."

The book's most prominent advocate was counterculture psychiatrist R.D. Laing, whose thinking on the positive functions of schizophrenic symptoms was highly influenced by the book. Two years after the arrival of *Operators and Things*, Laing released his seminal work, *The Divided Self* (1960) in which he posits his alternative views on mental illness – calling schizophrenia a reasonable response to an insane world.

While *Operators and Things* met with nearly universal acclaim, eventually there were a few detractors. In *Varieties of Psychopathological Experience* (1964), Carney Landis, Ph.D., raises his concerns about *Operators and Things*, calling it an "alleged" autobiographical account. He explains that the book is "in style and content quite different from the usual description of hallucinatory experiences that commonly involve ideas of persecution and religion, accompanied by fearful astonishment. In contrast, Miss O'Brien's description resembles modern science fiction more than any other we have encountered." In a footnote, Landis describes his unsuccessful attempts to contact the publisher to verify the book's validity. He concludes that it is his opinion, "*Operators and Things* should not be accepted at face value until something more tangible can be learned about the circumstances that gave rise to its writing and publication."

In the present day, we have seen many prominent examples of faked, embellished, or fraudulent memoirs and blogs. How can we believe with certainty that *Operators and Things* is the real thing? That was one of the reasons I wanted to talk with Michael Maccoby, the doctoral student, now psychoanalyst and established author, who in 1958 wrote the book's introduction. My conversation with Dr. Maccoby, which addresses a variety of topics, including the book's veracity, is the final entry in this volume.* In preparing this edition, I also contacted L. J. Reyna, Ph.D., who wrote the original preface, now ninety-three years old and living in Florida.

While I didn't end up adapting *Operators and Things* into a play, I did find myself going back to the book for another reason in the early 1990s. I'd recently collaborated with Colleen Delegan on a romantic comedy that won several screenwriting competitions. As we tossed around ideas for our next script, I realized we could adapt

---

* When I submitted this foreword to Dr. Maccoby for his review, he responded via email: "I hadn't known the impact of the book." (As Maccoby mentions in the interview at the end of this edition, around the time *Operators and Things* was originally published, he moved to Mexico, where he and his family lived for eight years while he worked with Erich Fromm.)

*Operators and Things* for the screen. We collaborated on the screenplay for about a year and copyrighted our adaptation in 1994.

Since that time, many people seeking information about Barbara O'Brien and her book have contacted us. Several individuals – including those from major Hollywood studios – have inquired about our screenplay. We have also received inquiries from people with intense interest in the book from either a literary or personal standpoint.

We received several emails from book archivist and magazine writer Robert Nedelkoff. In his blog, neglectedbooks.com, Nedelkoff includes *Operators and Things* on his list of the twelve most neglected books of all time. He says: "When I came across an Ace paperback edition of this book, published in the early 1960s, I at first thought I was reading one of Philip K. Dick's greatest achievements...I'm not sure that what is being described is not an extended psychotic episode of a schizoid nature with a spontaneous cure (or perhaps better phrased, an abatement) like the mathematician John Forbes Nash's. But it still is a very strange and dispassionately told book."

Another writer who saw a connection between O'Brien's book and Philip K. Dick's oeuvre was Laurence A. Rickels, author of *I Think I Am Philip K. Dick*. In his book, Rickels devotes and entire chapter to *Operators and Things*, using it as a counterpoint to Dick's *Vulcan's Hammer* (1960), which deals with a mad society.

These writers weren't the only ones who drew a parallel between *Operators and Things* and science fiction. Barbara makes the connection herself, stating: "Schizophrenics, long before writers dreamed up science fiction, had – as they still have – a consistent way of developing mental worlds filled with Men From Mars, devils, death-ray experts, and other fanciful characters."

Several books about alien encounters have cited *Operators and Things* as an example of visitations by beings from outside our planet. These books posit that Barbara did not experience a psychotic break, but rather abduction by alien "operators." Whether considered science fact, science fiction, or science something-else, writers of these books take their subject very seriously and cite Barbara as an alien-abduction alumna.

*Operators and Things* predated two better-known works that deal with women afflicted with mental illness – Joanne Greenberg's *I Never Promised You a Rose Garden* (1964) and Sylvia Plath's *The Bell Jar* (1963). But in 1951 – seven years before *Operators and Things* arrived – W.B. Saunders, a medical publisher, released *Autobiography of a Schizophrenic* Girl (1951) by the pseudonymous "Renee" – a book that noted novelist Frank Conroy in his foreword to an updated edition called "an astonishing tour de force of prose." Could Barbara have read or been familiar with this work? Could it have influenced *Operators and Things*?

In her inspired anthology entitled *Out of Her Mind: Women Writing on Madness* (2000), Rebecca Shannonhouse spent years searching out material by women who'd written nonfiction or fictional accounts of mental illness. These include Margery Kempe's 1436 tale of torment at the hands of the devil, letters by Zelda Fitzgerald written from an asylum, and other writings from the nineteenth and twentieth centuries. These accounts shed light on the particular challenges that have faced women deemed mentally ill – including institutionalization because they couldn't fit society's norms and sterilization to rid them of hysteria.

From my reading of *Operators and Things*, I figured Barbara must have been around thirty at the time the book was published in 1958 – meaning, she was probably born in the late 1920s. As of this writing, 2011, she would be in her early eighties – and, if she's still with us and reads these words, we want her to know how much her book has meant to so many people over the past fifty-plus years. She used a pseudonym and closely guarded her identity because she feared having to live with the stigma of "former mental patient." We hope that the current response to *Operators and Things* would cheer her. Reviews posted on websites of top online booksellers and blogs, reveal that readers have drawn inspiration and courage from Barbara's book, calling it, "Exciting," "fascinating," "incredible," "great," "spectacular," "entertaining," "thought-provoking," "brilliant," "remarkable," "classic," "profound," "astounding," and many other superlatives – with five-star reviews across the board.

Long out of print, we are reissuing *Operators and Things* to keep alive Barbara's beautiful work, as well as pay homage to her personal courage and artistry. The last time she revealed anything about herself was in 1976, when she wrote a new chapter for a paperback edition of the book. In the chapter, she shared a few details about herself – saying that just five people knew about her schizophrenia: agent, publisher, ex-husband, and two others.

For this edition, we wanted to create a mood of the times. It may be difficult for today's readers to understand what life was like more than fifty years ago, when people had no cell phones, no Internet, and rarely traveled by plane. In those days, people handwrote letters and put them in a mailbox, used phone booths, and traveled by train and Greyhound bus. To paint a picture of what life was like fifty-plus years ago, we've selected some classic images from the Library of Congress collection, including those by iconic photographers Esther Bubley, Russell Lee, and John Vachon. Especially poignant are Esther Bubley's photos of Greyhound buses taken in her role as a photographer with a government agency during World War II.

Putting this edition together has been a labor of love that we hope will draw a new generation to *Operators and Things*, Barbara O'Brien's influential, important work and an entertaining and enlightening one as well – everything a writer (or reader) could hope for from a piece of writing.

For those of you reading *Operators and Things* for the first time and for those taking the journey once again, bon voyage.

MELANIE VILLINES

# Introduction

"Everything about this psychology is, in the deepest sense, experience," C.G. Jung has written, "the entire theory, even when it puts on its most abstract airs, is the direct outcome of something experienced." Jung also writes, "To *experience* a dream and its interpretation is very different from having a tepid rehash set before you on paper."[1]

This book is one person's experience of living a dream which does not fit easily into abstract theory, even the author's own. As she tells us, the dry beach of the conscious mind is a poor relation to the unconscious. Although we speak a common conscious language, socialized by our common culture, it is no easy thing for a man to communicate with even his own unconscious. For psychology, everyone's experience must be relevant; the experts in this field depend on the experience of others. Theory is little more than an organizing myth, and myths become powerful theories only by remaining sensitive to experience.

Ideally, we would like to be able to apply the content of Barbara's schizophrenic world to some myth or model, no matter how inadequate, of the unconscious processes. In this connection, two points made by Barbara are particularly interesting to me. The first is her feeling that the drama staged by her unconscious was an attempt to save her from the unbearable, an idea that supports Freud's hypothesis that the hallucinatory (hysterical) mechanism is

---

[1] C.G. Jung, *Two Essays on Analytical Psychology*, New York: Meridian, 1956. Page 127. The essay, "General Remarks on the Therapeutic Approach to the Unconscious," of which this quotation is a part, is particularly relevant to Barbara's account of her hallucinations. Jung, much more so than Freud, is aware of the healing and creative as well as the destructive elements in the unconscious.

an attempt at recovery, not the disease itself.[2] Barbara's hallucinations are not, however, the gods and devils common to another age; they are horrors of Organization Man; they are reactions to forces blocking attempts at creativity in work and attempts to enjoy relationships of trust with others.

Those who are creative in Barbara's world are impaled by the hook and those who trust are removed. For most of us, these problems of creativity and intimacy are the difference between a meaningful and satisfying life as opposed to a life of quiet desperation. To Barbara, they are matters of staying alive, and this is perhaps as good a way as any to state simply the difference between the meaning of a problem to a normal person and to a schizophrenic. As Barbara admits honestly, her problems are not solved; she cannot claim a complete cure. The hallucinations are gone and her conscious mind can hold down a job; but the hook operators are still unbearable, and there is no indication that she can trust enough to *enjoy* human contact.

In fact, she tells little of her feelings about the people who are and were significant in her life. The only interactions we witness (other than her hallucinatory dramas) are her contacts with a busy, uncaring psychiatrist and with a caricature of an "orthodox" psychoanalyst, who seems alternately amazed at Barbara's unconscious (understandably so) and intrigued by her femininity (a Frenchman, he suggests be with an experienced European lover as a cure, an idea that Barbara wisely considers would create, for her, more problems than it would solve). For Barbara, the world

---

[2] Sigmund Freud, "On the Mechanism of Paranoia," in *Collected Papers Volume III*, London: The Hogarth Press, 1925. Pages 444-470. In fact, Freud credits the idea of hallucinations as attempts at recovery to Jung's observations that the flight of ideas and motor stereotypes occurring in this disorder (dementia praecox or paraphrenia) are the relics of former object-cathexes, clung to with convulsive energy.

Barbara places herself in the diagnostic category of paranoia. It is probably more correct to call her illness *paraphrenia*, which, as Freud points out, is close to paranoia and can develop from it. The differences are described briefly in the above paper. This paper is worth reading from another angle, also. Barbara's description of the "cure" offered by the psychoanalyst she saw is quite different from Freud's theories about paraphrenia and its aeteosis, which he considers less sexual in the normal sense, more related to early infant problems which might better be called problems of trust and autonomy.

remains hostile; survival is the central problem. The only optimistic elements in the story are Barbara's considerable intelligence and the creative urge which led to her novel and to this book.

Psychology does not know much about creativity. Freud analyzes Dostoevsky as a neurotic, but he admits: "Before the problem of the creative artist analysis must, alas, lay down its arms."[3] In a similar way, one can explain William Blake's hallucinations and his denunciations of the Royal Academy's Hook Operators, but the music of Blake's words, the form of their content, and the fact of creativity, rather than stagnation, remain an awesome mystery. Barbara writes and she writes well; creativity is a therapy by which Barbara transcends the psychiatrists' work-a-day world of confessions and standardized inkblots. She imposes regularity and form over chaos, socializing the unconscious language in a way only the best therapies ever approach. Yet, as I have said, there is a great distance between bare survival and a satisfying life.

Barbara gives us another idea which has to do with some of the most interesting research into the connection between mental illness and physiological imbalance. She feels that her unconscious presented her with a drama with at least one moral to it: get your adrenal working, get angry or you will destroy yourself. Recent research indicates that depressive psychotics and some schizophrenics (indeed some normal-neurotics) who react to stress with fear show a different physiological pattern to stress than do those who react with anger or cunning. For example, those who fear (the anger-in people as Funkenstein[4] calls them) secrete less nor-adrenalin. Perhaps the anger-in people fear the feeling of anger itself more than they fear retaliation by real others. Perhaps the reaction of fear is a physiological poison which threatens a person's life. Perhaps only a psychological change, a willingness to be angry,

---

[3] Sigmund Freud, "Dostoevsky and Parricide," in *Collected Papers, Volume V*, London: Hogarth Press, 1950.

[4] D.H. Funkenstein, S.H. King and M.E. Drolette, *Mastery of Stress*, Cambridge: Harvard University Press, 1957.

can support a physiological reorganization. It is also possible that the fear of being angry spreads to become the fear of doing anything active which becomes he wish to crawl into a hole. Barbara's mad dash across the country seems to be like a first step toward curative activity as well as the abandonment of an environment from which her mind has already fled.

If the reader shares my curiosity, he or she will have the wish to know more about Barbara. What does she look like? What was her childhood like? What is she doing now? What kind of people have been important to her, other than people in authority? All we know is that she is a creative and independent woman, with intelligence, a strong sense of morality, and a talent for playfulness. Her playfulness and humor is to me Barbara's most impressive quality. Faced with a matter of life and death which lasted not for a moment but for months, her unconscious produced, along with Kafkaesque judges and Edward G. Robinson-type gangsters, characters like Nicky who are warm and playful. This book itself has an element of a Hollywood script, but a script which illustrates man's most endearing quality, the ability to translate the dangers within him, the fears about good and evil, into an external drama with heroes and villains, with pathos and humor.[5] Psychology, if it is to science rather than dogma, must learn from people like Barbara that the unconscious is not at all like the mechanized models of human behavior upon which we depend all too much.

MICHAEL MACCOBY
*Harvard University*

---

[5] For a discussion of the value of man's playfulness and his ability to "reflect fearlessly on the strange customs and institutions by which...(he) must find self-realization," see Erik H. Erikson, Childhood and Society, New York: W.W. Norton and Col, 1950, particularly the chapter "The Fear of Anxiety." One of Erikson's observations helps me to understand Barbara's case in a way different form the approach taken by Barbara herself. Barbara reports that her greatest fear from the operators is that of being dummetized, being made empty. And she finally believes that this has happened. Erikson writes: "The fear of being left empty, and, more simply, that of being left, seems to be the most basic feminine fear, extending over the whole of a woman's existence. It is normally intensified with every menstruation and takes its final toll during the menopause. No wonder, then, that the anxiety aroused by these fears can express itself either in complete subjugation to male thought, in desperate competition with it, or in efforts to catch the male and make him a mere tool." Page 366.

# Prefatory Note

In this book, an intelligent, observant, and talented woman returns from a world of hallucinatory characters to join therapists and researchers in their pursuit of the causes of schizophrenia.

In her attempt to understand how she suddenly enters this world and emerged after six months from it, the author presents a startlingly clear account of our present state of knowledge and ignorance about schizophrenia. Her detailed and systematic report and interpretation of her illness and recovery provide a valuable and rich source of data and hypotheses which will place researchers in mental illness in her debt.

I believe that not only will professionals regard this work as an outstanding contribution to studies on the etiology, treatment and sociology of mental illness, but that all readers will view this work as brilliant literature and see in it the emergence of an artist.

L.J. REYNA
*Research Consultant, V.A. Hospital, Bedford, Massachusetts*
*Associate Professor of Psychology, Boston University*

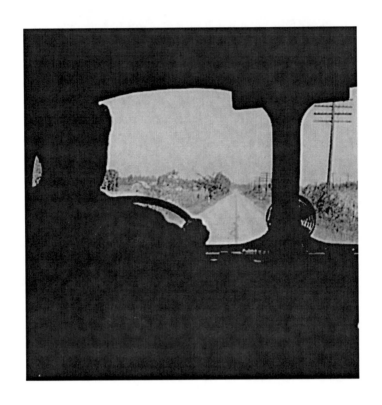

# Schizophrenia: The Demon in Control

Let us say that when you awake tomorrow, you find standing at your bedside a man with purple scale-skin who tells you that he has just arrived from Mars, that he is studying the human species, and that he has selected your mind for the kind of on-the-spot examination he wants to make.

While you are catching your breath he walks casually to your best chair, drapes his tail over it, and informs you that he will be visible and audible only to you. Fixing his three eyes sternly upon you, he warns you not to reveal his presence; if you attempt to do so, he threatens, he will kill you instantly.

You may wonder, perhaps, if you are sane. But the Man From Mars is standing before you, clear and colorful, and his voice is loud and distinct. On the basis of what you can so clearly see and hear, you accept the fact, astounding as it is, that the stranger is what he says he is.

If your temperament were such that you would not be able to accept the fact that a Man From Mars might just pop into your room, the vision appearing before you would not be a Man From Mars. It might be, instead, the awesome figure of God. Or the terrifying figure of the devil. Or it might be a much less conventional figure. In all probability the figure, regardless of the form it took, would have three characteristics: it would represent authority; it would have superhuman powers; and its weirdness would, in some way, seem plausible and acceptable to you.

Let us say that you are faced with the Man From Mars and that prior unresolved speculations concerning flying saucers give the figure a certain plausibility. You are rattled but you attempt to go through your normal activities, keeping your tremendous secret to yourself. You converse with your friends, perform your job, and eat your meals, even while the figure stands at your side. The Man

From Mars advises you that it is not necessary to answer his questions, that you need only to think your answers, for he will be able to read your mind. You find this is no idle boast; the Man proceeds to demonstrate his ability to do just that.

If you are sufficiently controlled you may carry your secret around with you for some time before anyone suspects that something unusual has happened to you. A friend may notice that you seem somewhat distraught and suggest that you unburden your troubles. You ignore his advice. Obviously, such an action would result only in the instant death of you and your confidant. Instead, you become more careful of your behavior, hold onto yourself with everything you've got, and pray desperately for the Man From Mars to complete his research and depart.

It is possible that the Man From Mars may actually disappear within a few days or a few weeks. There is about a .05 per cent chance of this happening. You are physically exhausted after the Man has gone back to Mars, and your mind, which had been racing like a jet plane while the Man was with you, slows down and almost refuses to function at all. But as the days pass, you gradually revert to normalcy. In time, you may discuss your experience with some one and you may even discover, at this point, what was really happening to you while the Man From Mars was with you.

There is a 99.95 per cent chance, however, if something like the Man From Mars appears in your life, that he is still in your life after a few months. By that time it is very probable that you are in a mental institution, undergoing periodic electric or insulin shock treatment. There is a chance of the Man's disappearing after a few shock treatments.

There is a much better chance that the Man is still with you after the hundredth dose of shock. By that time you may become so demoralized that you don't care whether the Man kills you or not; or the doctors may inject drugs which induce you to talk. You find yourself eagerly telling the doctors and anyone else whose ear you can capture about your visitor and his purpose in haunting you.

They don't believe you. This doesn't altogether surprise you. After all, other people can't see and hear the Man; he's not tuned in on them. The Man may get nasty after your revelation of his presence and you may get angry enough to take a few punches at him—and feel jubilant about doing just this. While you are glorying in this first release of your months-old tension, you find that you are being fitted snugly into a restraining jacket and that strong tranquilizing drugs are being stuffed down your throat, or that the shock treatments have been increased to reduce your aggressiveness.

The tranquilizers or the shock therapy have the desired effect and your impulse to challenge the Man disappears. You review your situation despondently and finally resign yourself to the inevitable, realizing that there isn't a thing any human being in the world can do for you. You wait wearily for the Man to go back to Mars. You might be in the institution for the rest of your life and the Man From Mars might be there with you.

You have a common variety of the mental disease, schizophrenia, a mental disorder more prevalent in America than it is anywhere else and one which is mounting in rate of increase with each year. Your mind is "split," and a subconscious portion of it, no longer under your conscious control, is staging a private show for your benefit. The kind of show it stages will depend upon the kind of stuff that is in it and upon the relationship that existed between your conscious and unconscious while your mind was whole. It may, with each passing day, tear you to smaller and smaller pieces. It may, on the other hand, patiently stitch together the segments of you that have split apart.

One thing is certain: when you sit on your ward bench, staring at the wall, studying your apparition and despondently concluding that no other human being in the world can help you, your deduction will be a sane and reasonable one. If you develop schizophrenia which cannot be arrested by a few doses of shock therapy or tranquilizers, then there is no other human being in the world who can help you. The only thing that can help you at that point is the demon in control, your own unconscious mind.

According to statistics released by the National Association for Mental Health, your chance of being hospitalized for a severe mental illness during your lifetime is, in 1957, if you are an American, 1 in 12. In 1946, it was 1 in 16; in 1936, it was 1 in 20.

An 11 out of 12 chance of escaping insanity is not too bad. The odds are not as good as 19 out of 20. However, they are considerably better than the 4 out of 5 chance which seems to be looming on the horizon for 1976.

If you are the unlucky 1 in 12, there is a 60 per cent to 70 per cent chance that the mental disease you develop is a variety of schizophrenia. It is the mounting rate of increase in this one mental disorder which is crowding every mental institution in this country.

Just why schizophrenia should be the great insanity trap for the American emotional make-up is not certain. Nor is it by any means certain that schizophrenia is emotional in origin. It may, or it may not, be the result of unbearable environmental pressures. It may, or it may not, be the result of endocrine gland disorders. Or it may be the result of a diet lacking in sufficient amino acids or some other substance. All of these theories are being explored by the medium-sized garret of research psychiatrists who are trying to determine the cause of the disease.

There are only three facts which are really certain about schizophrenia at this time: no one knows what causes it; no one knows how to cure it; the number of research psychiatrists who are presently attempting to determine the cause and the cure of the disease is so small that the chance of their coming upon the solution in the near future is relatively poor.

At the rate at which schizophrenia is increasing, there is a reasonable chance that if the intercontinental missile doesn't get you, schizophrenia will. Your chances of being hit by a flying missile haven't yet been determined, although your chances of remaining intact, if hit, may be surmised. Your chances of being hit by schizophrenia in the immediate future are higher, and your chances of making a comeback, if hit, aren't much better.

There is an amazing lack of accurate knowledge among laymen concerning the effects of schizophrenia upon its victims. The most prevalent current notion is that, when the mind is split in schizophrenia, the individual becomes two people, two distinct personalities, or even multiple personalities—that the subconscious mind, rebelling against the repressions imposed upon it, has declared civil war, deserted the conscious authority; and that in the resulting schism, the new personality which emerges periodically is composed of the parts of the personality which the individual has consciously, deliberately, persistently repressed.

In infrequent cases, this appears to be just what does happen. The unconscious has rebelled, assumed control, created the person it wishes to be, forced the conscious controller into a small, tightly closed box where it cannot even see what is going on, and then taken over the floor of the conscious mind.

In most cases of schizophrenia, however, the unconscious appears to prefer not the techniques of the actor, but those of the director. It does not create a new personality but, instead, stages a play. The major difference is that the conscious mind is permitted to remain, an audience of one sitting lonely in the theater, watching a drama on which it cannot walk out.

Even though the circumstances which induce or permit the unconscious mind to rise and take over are still a mystery, the fact that in schizophrenia it rises to do just that is strikingly clear. As you sit watching your Martian, it is your unconscious mind which is flashing the picture before your eyes, sounding the Man's voice in your ears. More than this, it is blowing a fog of hypnosis over your conscious mind so that consciously you are convinced that the hallucinations you see and hear and the delusions that accompany the hallucinations are real.

In sanity you would know, if the apparition of a Man From Mars appeared before you, that you were having a hallucination. An alcoholic in the throes of delirium tremens, watching tigers walking around his living room, knows that they are not tigers, knows that they are hallucinations, and knows also what has caused the hallucinations to appear. In schizophrenia, an important part of your reasoning mechanism has been fogged by something which normally is the most cooperative assistant your conscious mind could desire, your subconscious mental cellar, your unconscious—

what an unsuitable name for it!—mind.

Your court of last resort, in schizophrenia, appears to be this unconscious mind of yours, the demon in control. However it manages to get its hands on the throttle, its behavior in the initial stages of control leaves no doubt about what it is up to. Without even stopping for a deep breath, it gets its Martian, or whatever, going. With speed and apparent purposefulness, it escorts the conscious mind to a box seat, makes it comfortable, and projects the shape or shapes it has created, and the voice or voices it has chosen. As it does so, it wafts a little suggestive breeze in the direction of the box seat. "Believe what you hear," says the little breeze; "believe what you see. These things are real, or else they could not be."

The figure which is projected in front of your eyes may be wispy and ghostlike, or nontransparent, or even multicolored. Schizophrenics have reported all varieties. You may have a fair technician, or a good technician, or a technician-artist in your sub-cellar. The voice which accompanies the shape is always convincingly loud and distinct, the voice business being apparently a quite simple technical achievement for unconscious talents. Having bolstered itself with the props it needs, the unconscious then proceeds to do what it has apparently created the props to effect—it begins to give you directions.

Even in the last outposts of schizophrenia, your conscious mind retains certain prerogatives; behind all the props and trappings devised by the unconscious is the unconscious realization that the conscious mind must be induced, cajoled, threatened into line. Clearly your conscious mind has been devised to rule and command, and your unconscious is acutely aware of the fact. In charge, it draws upon every bit of business it can concoct to keep you bamboozled.

What sort of directions docs it give you? Well, that depends. The unconscious is, whatever else it is, the repository of whatever you have put into it during your lifetime. Statistics indicate that all sorts of people get schizophrenia. You may be male or female, young or old, brilliant or stupid, rich or poor, stable or unstable, a good guy or a bad guy, and still wake up some morning to find the Man From Mars at your bedside. This is one of the mysteries of schizophrenia. Your Man may be amazingly constructive in the advice he gives you. On the other hand, he may aim you, like an arrow, to destroy everything and anything, including yourself. Self-cures are not uncommon in schizophrenia. Neither are suicides and murders. There is a terrible kind of ironic justice in schizophrenia. Whatever it is you are, you are, possibly for the first time in your life, at the absolute mercy of.

What sort of people have become schizophrenics? The variety has been infinite. There is a good chance that Joan of Arc was a schizophrenic. The shrewd peasant perceptivity that looked out upon a broken, demoralized country and saw how it could be healed and revitalized might well have been unconscious. That it fooled conscious Joan as completely as it fooled a nation is undoubted. Joan saw and heard the conventional figures of saints and followed their directions. Behind her flying banner and her vision, a defeated people came to life. (Whether or not Joan was an instrument of God is beside the point. I would assume that Joan's sainthood could run parallel to her schizophrenia. The hand of God is large and its lines are complex.)

On the other hand, the man who a few years ago murdered his mother-in-law at the direction of his "voices" was a schizophrenic. In a way, he is easier to understand than Joan. He did what a great many people have wished to do. Poor Joan looked out on a broken country and under the strain, her mind split. But what came from the rift was a whole thing, a desire to serve many people.

Between Joan and the mother-in-law murderer there have been a million shapes and shades. It is possible, even probable, many think, that Bridey Murphy was the concoction of an unconscious mind which gained a freedom in hypnosis similar to the freedom it gains in schizophrenia. At its best, it was displaying a desire to cooperate and please; at its worst, it was no more than impish as it plotted its story of Bridey and waited for the next moment to perform. Certainly, Mrs. Simmons had no more idea than Joan of what was going on in the sub-cellar.

I developed schizophrenia abruptly, in the way which is now considered most fortunate for an optimistic prognosis, I awoke one morning, during a time of great personal tension and self conflict, to find three grey and somewhat wispy figures standing at my bedside. I was, as might be imagined, completely taken up by them. Within a few minutes they had banished my own sordid problem from my mind and replaced it with another and more intriguing one. They were not Men From Mars, but the Operators, a group in some ways stranger than Martians could be. I listened to what the Operators had to say, weighed the facts which they presented to me, and decided that there was wisdom in following their directions. I packed some clothes and mounted a Greyhound bus, as they directed, and followed them. Riding off in the bus, I left safely behind me a mess of reality with which I was totally incapable of coping.

But what I could not face in sanity, I had to face in insanity. It became clear in time that the problem presented to me by the Operators was exactly the problem I had left behind me. Caught up in my new world, and with the world of sanity almost wiped from my mind, the resemblance between the two worlds was not apparent until afterward—six months afterward, when I walked into a psychoanalyst's office at the advice of my voices, and gave him the message they had told me to give him. To his trained eye, the evidences of an approaching spontaneous recovery were apparent. He sweated out a four-day period waiting for it to occur. Just as he had almost given up hope, major symptoms—"the voices"—abruptly disappeared.

In sanity I had been a trained observer with an excellent memory, and in insanity my abilities had remained with me. Recovered and sane again, I was able to recall even the small motions, the whispers, of my demon while it had stood at the controls, I had sat placidly enough in my box seat during insanity, relaxed, and in a way enjoying the play. The play had seemed to have a purpose and after a fashion I had finally gotten the point. By the time I wandered into the analyst's office I knew, and knew well, what the score was.

That I was one of the lucky ones who went through the processes of self-cure gives the story of the Operators certain values. Sharp, Hinton, the Hook Operators, even the Spider as he scalloped out the latticework, were busy at the job of healing a rift in the mental machinery. They were strange gangsters to have been engaged in a constructive enterprise, but the unconscious which devised them had several things in mind, not the least being a desire to hold the interest of the customer in the box seat.

The chapters in this book which deal with the Operators relate an authentic account of schizophrenia, shortened considerably, but unchanged. This is a sample of what goes on in a schizophrenic mind. The chapters which deal with the period immediately following my recovery from major symptoms contain material which is, in some ways, even stranger than the conversations of the Operators. Some of these incidents, considered separately, are strange indeed. But considered as a group, they are apparent for what they are. The mental machinery was still mending, and the conscious mind was still incapable of taking over the total direction of the whole machine. Until it was ready, the unconscious stepped in, as was necessary, to guide, direct, and ease the way. Possibly because its wilder talents were easier to use when emergencies arose, it occasionally used such talents. When the machine was healed and the conscious mind was at the controls again, the weird incidents ceased. The conscious mind had never welcomed them, had frequently been disturbed by them, and was considerably relieved when they stopped.

The chapters which have to do with the two business firms in which I was employed have been camouflaged, to the best of my ability, without destroying in any way the essence of the emotional environment with which both were permeated. I have no desire to embarrass the individuals with whom I worked or the companies which employed me. There is, as a matter of fact, nothing startling or unusual about the environment in either office. Both are typical of the present-day scene.

And so is schizophrenia.

# Part One
# The Operators Leave

The Operators left me at the door of the analyst's office just as they had on my prior visits.

Dr. Donner was standing in the middle of his office waiting for me. Uneasiness hung around the room like a thick mist. He's been walking up and down, I thought, spraying worry around. The room is filled with worry.

He smiled and motioned me to the couch. I sat and waited for him to explain about the worry.

"I've been discussing your case with an associate." He waved an arm vaguely and looked away at one of the walls, and the fixed, amiable expression on his face collapsed. His face suddenly looked worn and tired, and somewhat fearful. Something has him scared, I thought, and leaned forward to study his face.

"Schizophrenia rarely clears up after this length of time without shock therapy." He walked to his desk and looked at a little notebook that lay open, "You're sure of the date when it started?"

Yes, I was quite sure.

"It's been six months." He brooded at the wall. "I don't like shock treatment. It isn't effective in most cases, and sometimes the results are—are not desirable." The fear on his face was quite clear now.

Then I realized why I was studying his face so closely. Hinton was tuned in on my mind and was studying the analyst's face through my eyes.

"I'm afraid it will have to be a hospital." The doctor seemed to remember something. He stopped brooding at the wall and turned around and looked at me carefully. "I was really hoping— there were such sharp indications . . ." He seemed to be waiting for me to say something.

Plunge right in, the Operators had taught me. Plunge right in and tackle it, whatever it is, "When do I go?" I asked.

Dr. Donner sighed. Then he turned a page of his notebook and asked me for the names and addresses of close relatives. Yes, they all were thousands of miles away. No, I didn't know anybody at all in this city. He wrote carefully in his notebook. I was to come back to his office the next day at the same time and he would come with me to the hospital.

I left and waited outside the building. I waited a full five minutes but neither Hinton nor Hazel came. There hadn't been much point in telling Dr. Donner that Hinton and Hazel would really make the decision about my going to the hospital. They had been arguing all night about how my head should be repaired. Their voices had still been snapping at each other when I had fallen asleep.

Hazel wanted me to get my head repaired but she recommended only one method: covering my head with stone. Stone, she said, would prevent Operators from tuning in on my mind. Hinton was opposed to stone.

"What's wrong with stone," Hazel had asked him. "A good thick coat of stone will mean safety. The latticework will grow in fine and there won't be any danger that some busybody Operator will fiddle around with the latticework while it is growing in."

"That's what I'm talking about," Hinton had shot back at her. "I want to get at the latticework when it's growing in. I want to make certain that it grows in right. No stone. It's got to be board and peephole."

Personally, I was in favor of stone. I knew what latticework was. It was the Operators' term for habit patterns. My habit patterns had been scalloped out and they had to grow back again. And I didn't want a screwball like Hinton supervising the growth of my habit patterns.

I looked at my wristwatch. They always had picked me up as soon as I left the doctor's office. I went back to the hotel, opened the door to my room and listened. Nothing. I went in and sat down and waited. Finally, I went to bed. As soon as I awoke and saw the clock, I knew they weren't around. The Operators never allowed me to sleep more than six hours. I had slept fifteen hours.

Dr. Donner was in his office looking much the same as he had the day before. He doesn't know, I thought. His Operator may know but he doesn't know. "They're gone," I told him. "The voices. They went away and they didn't come back."

The doctor's mouth sagged and then snapped suddenly and stretched into a wide smile, He took a deep breath and then smiled again and asked me to sit down and to tell him all about it. His head nodded happily as I talked.

"Will they be back?" I asked.

He threw a knife-sharp look at me as if he thought I might be trying to warn him of something. Then he stepped in and took charge. He hadn't been in charge until then. He just had been sitting around the same way I had been, waiting to see what the Operators would do. He stood up very tall and looked very confident.

"No. No. They won't be back. You won't have to go to a hospital. We won't have to use shock therapy. You're going to be all right." He threw another sharp look at me to see if I were observing how confident he was. He went back to his desk and shoved papers around and looked as if he were decidedly in charge of everything.

"No hospital," he said very confidently.

No stone, I thought, no stone.

"We're going to use psychoanalysis," Dr. Donner said.

The board and peephole, I thought, and I realized that Hinton had won.

Dr. Donner surprised me. I had always imagined that psychoanalysts presented a calm, serene facade to their patients, a bulwark against which all emotions could break without leaving a dent. Dr. Donner was impatient, sensitive, jumpy. I observed but did not absorb his impatience. Since the voices of the Operators had disappeared, I had been empty and dry, an automaton without emotion, almost without thought. Peace had finally come to me after months of the bedlam of the Operators, a gabby crowd if ever there were one, and the quiet beach of my mind was at rest.

I LOOKED CAREFULLY AT THE SWAN. ANOTHER WAVE
BROKE ON THE SAND. I ABSORBED IT AND TRANSLATED IT, "IT'S HIS LEG," I
SAID. "MAYBE IT'S SORE AND THE WATER IS IRRITATING IT, OR ELSE THE
SWAN IS JUST RESTING IT."

"Did you read fantasy fiction?" Dr. Donner asked. "The Operators sound like characters created by a writer of fantasies."

My memories of the Operators were sharp as icicles but searching through the past of sanity was like picking up rocks, every effort devastating. I said, finally, "I used to read *Time*. I tried to read the *Evening Times* every night but I didn't always have the time. I didn't have the time, even, to always read *Time*." The repetition of the word delighted me. I wanted more of it. "You might say," I added, "that I didn't have the time to take advantage of the time."

He tried again. "You exercised remarkable self-control, traveling around the country the way you did for six months— considering the condition you were in."

I stifled the impulse to tell him that his statement was absurd. I hadn't been in control. I had been controlled. I said, because I wondered if he had doubts about it, "I want you to understand that all the flukey-lukey has stopped. I'm perfectly all right now." Except that my head was so dry and so empty.

"You've gotten rid of major symptoms. You realize that you had schizophrenic hallucinations and that the Operators did not exist. By the way, why do you refer to your delusions as 'flukey-lukey'?"

I stared blankly. Why did I?

"Think about it a moment," he said irritably. "Don't say there is nothing going on in your mind. You say that very often. But there is always mental action going on somewhere in the mind."

I tried to think but the effort hurt and I rested. A gentle wave broke on the dry beach of my mind: my mind is resting because it needs rest more than it needs an analyst at this point. I was about to put the gentle wave into words when another wave flooded softly over the shore: it would not be wise to say this. I stared and was silent.

The analyst looked at his clock, took out his notebook, scheduled me for another appointment, and waited while I laboriously copied the time and date on a piece of paper.

I went directly to the park where I was now spending most of my time. The park was large and peaceful. In its center was a lake on whose waters ducks, gulls, mud fowl, and one large swan went about their daily routine of living. I had always liked birds but had never found much time to watch them. Time was all about me now.

The swan glided across the lake and on its back was a long, black rod. The woman sitting on the bench beside me leaned forward. "Will you look at that swan," she said. "There's some kind of stick on its back."

I looked carefully at the swan. Another wave broke on the sand. I absorbed it and translated it, "It's his leg," I said. "Maybe it's sore and the water is irritating it, or else the swan is just resting it."

She peered over the water. "Oh, yes, I see now," she said.

I was delighted with the waves. They were soft and gentle and they brought useful information into the dry empty cavern of my head. I should never have known about the long black stick being a swan's leg. I had never seen a swan before. I walked to the lake for a closer look.

The swan's leg still looked like a black stick. I was a bit dubious about its being his leg, but I trusted the waves. The waves were far more clever than the dry beach.

I watched the birds for hours. They help keep the Operators away, I thought, A wave cascaded gently on the beach: I must remember, not flukey-lukey, but schizophrenia; not Operators, but my unconscious mind; everything the Operators had said to me, my unconscious had said to my conscious mind. I watched the birds and something that wasn't a wave stirred on the dry beach. How very odd, I mused, that my unconscious mind should call itself an Operator and call my conscious mind a Thing.

I WAS NEW TO BUSINESS AND I WAS CONCERNED, AS ARE
A CONSIDERABLE NUMBER OF YOUNG WOMEN WHEN
THEY START TO WORK, IN DISCOVERING THE ANSWER TO
"HOW DO I GET INTO THE BIG SALARY CLASS?"

# Before the Operators Came

Whenever I think of the Hook Operators now, I see a picture of a man with a hook stuck in his back. The hook is attached to a rope and the rope hangs from a ceiling. At the end of the rope, unable to get his feet on solid ground, the man dangles in the air, his face distorted in agony, his arms and legs thrashing about violently.

Behind him stands the Hook Operator. Having operated his hook successfully, the Hook Operator stands by with his other instruments, the knife and the hatchet. He watches the thrashing man, speculating, considering, If necessary, he will move in and cut the victim's throat, or with his hatchet cleave through the victim's head.

The Hook Operator is a maker of tools and if he is an expert toolmaker, the hook alone will serve his purpose. The victim, in his thrashing to be free of the hook, will most likely cut into his back the crippling gorge the Hook Operator seeks. The Hook Operator waits and watches. What a man will do, once he is caught on the hook, is always a gamble. There is the chance, of course, that the man may squirm off the hook, in which case the Hook Operator will move in with his other weapons.

There is, too, the chance that the victim may accomplish more than the Hook Operator strives for and crack his backbone or, giving an unexpected twist to his thrashing, tear himself completely in two. Should break or schism occur, the Hook Operator as much as anyone may pause in distress, surveying a wreckage he did not seek and for which he feels no guilt. When he hooks, cuts, or cleaves, his object is not to destroy but to impede and remove. Not personal animosity but competition has impelled him to use his weapons. The man on the hook was not an enemy but an obstacle. Even had the Hook Operator cut his competitor's throat he would have cut it sufficiently but no more; had he cleaved his skull, he would have cleaved it just enough. Of his weapons, the hook is considered the least barbaric, the one which requires the most skill and the one for which he will receive the least censure.

The hook's purpose is to catch and upset, and it was designed for no other purpose. If the man on the hook receives more injury than was intended, he obviously received it by trying too obstinately to regain his balance on ground he should have forsaken, or by losing inner balance in falling into a frenzy he should have had the strength to avoid. Nor will the spectators watching on the outskirts of the circle be inclined to condemn the Hook Operator if tragedy, instead of upset, occurs. The hook is the commonly accepted instrument of the circle where the Hook Operator works, a state of affairs which should have been clear to the victim as soon as he walked into the circle.

Considering the amount of hook operating that goes on in business organizations, it is surprising how little understanding of it exists among young people before they enter business. My own education for business was thorough enough, but I never had a course on "How to Recognize Hook Operating When You See It." Even a short lecture would have been helpful: it would have brought into focus a picture for my memory to store away. As it was, I had to attempt to fit pieces of a jigsaw puzzle together without any guide and without much notion of what the picture was going to be when it was completed.

I went to work for the Knox Company for the same reason that a great many other people did. Knox was mushrooming overnight into a big company, profits were high, and the rich, oily smell of money hung over the plant.

I was new to business and I was concerned, as are a considerable number of young women when they start to work, in discovering the answer to "How do I get into the big salary class?" With all that money around, and with the technical background I had, there seemed to be a reasonable chance that I might latch on to some of it. Almost immediately an answer of sorts developed right in front of me.

I had been working only a few days when the company announced that a new design department would be opened within a month, and that a young fellow named Ken Ryers, a pleasant, soft-spoken chap who sat a few desks away from me and who had been working for Knox less than a year, would be promoted to the position of manager of the new department.

The thing I recall most vividly about Ken was that his head was always buried in his blotter, and that if you wanted to get his attention, you had to stand almost on top of him and speak very loudly. "It's just that he concentrates hard," his girl used to say of him. "He actually forgets everything except what he's doing. Maybe that's why he turns out so much work."

I remember that I looked at the dark head that was always buried in a desk blotter and thought, "That's how it's done. It's simple and sweet. You sit at your desk and keep turning it out. If you're just a little better and if you turn it out for eight hours a day instead of the six hours a day that most people are willing to give, you're made."

The picture of hard working Ken getting a big promotion after only a short time with Knox had the kind of clear illustrative quality you see in the graphs in junior high school books, drawn in clear broad lines, and painted in bright lollipop colors. The picture was easy to understand and, I decided, not at all difficult to follow through on. I could see myself, within a few years, with a big fat salary, vacationing in Europe and writing postcards from Paris.

I found myself looking up frequently at Ken's dark head and feeling grateful to him for getting me started so early on the right track. Perhaps it was because I looked at Ken so often that I became aware that someone else was doing the same thing, a little pasty-faced fellow who sat on the other side of the room. His name was Gordon and he smoked a great deal, not nervously, but deliberately and slowly, as if he were testing and evaluating each cigarette.

Some thirty days later, when the new design department was opened and Gordon was installed as department manager, I was one of many who walked around with blank faces and raised eyebrows. One of the girls, in a hurried whisper, gave me as clear an answer as I was able to get for some time.

"Ken said something terrible about Knox Senior, It must have been really awful because nobody can find out what he said. Knox called Ken in and had it out with him and Ken got mad and said Knox was crazy for believing such trash. One word led to another and Ken really let loose. He's all washed up now."

I wondered, because of a subconscious irritation rather than any objective reason, how much Gordon knew about the story that had reached Knox Senior and started the explosion, No one was going to learn much from Ken. He kept his head buried in his blotter and kept his business to himself. No one was going to learn much from Gordon, either. He sat at the manager's desk in the new design department, smoking his slow cigarettes, and if he caught you looking at him his eyes would fix on your face in a cold, spiderish stare.

I've made some sharp revisions in my ideas of how people get ahead fast in business since the day I looked at Ken and saw how clear it all was. The thing you need is a special kind of skill that Ken didn't have and could never have developed. It's the technique of the Hook Operator.

Many people are horrified when they come upon hook operating, and their first reaction is, "That's something I could never stoop to doing." But, actually, the reason that a great many people don't become Hook Operators is because it's not at all easy to be one. They're clever, the Hook Operators, and ingenious and resourceful, and they give every bit of their talent and energy to the business of hook operating. To understand a Hook Operator, it is best to study him from the first clay that he sets his nimble, cloven foot inside the door of an organization.

A Hook Operator has a nose for power, and as soon as he enters an organization, he follows his nose until he comes upon the individual who is giving off the strongest odor. Having spotted him, the Hook Operator feels out the Powerman for his soft spot until he knows the exact location of the spot and its degree of softness.

There is value in taking a sharp look at this soft spot, for its nature is the one element that makes the career of the Hook Operator possible. If the Powerman doesn't have this kind of soft spot, the Hook Operator will get nowhere, but generally the Hook Operator has little to worry about on this score. Where there is power there is usually the kind of soft spot the Hook Operator is seeking. The soft spot is a simple thing, a hidden sense of insecurity. Its owner is so sharply aware of this soft spot that he keeps it hidden in a little box where he doesn't have to look at it and be aware of it. About this soft spot, however, the owner is so touchy that the slightest indication that someone suspects its existence will drive him crazy. The Hook Operator usually locates the soft spot very quickly, for this is part of his business; not giving any indication that he sees it is part of his technique.

As soon as he has gotten the soft spot in focus, the Hook Operator visualizes it as a target and shapes a weapon which will pierce that feeling of insecurity so that it will bleed for days. He then looks about to locate the guy-on-the-way-up, since this fellow will hold or will be credited with holding the weapon, and will throw or be credited with throwing it at the target.

There is a choice of techniques at this point. If the Hook Operator can manage it, the most effective method is to get the guy-on-the-way-up to actually throw the weapon. First, the Hook Operator studies the guy-on-the-way-up to locate his soft spot. If it exists, it will show itself under the Hook Operator's careful probing. Brought under the microscope, it is a rather soft, small, flabby thing, a feeling in the guy-on-the-way-up that he is not sufficiently appreciated by management.

Once he has brought this soft spot into focus, the Hook Operator pokes at it until it has grown to maximum size. When the Hook Operator has achieved this, a change becomes apparent in the guy-on-the-way-up. His fellow employees notice it and management notices it and they say, especially the members of management, that so-and-so's personal morale is not what it used to be.

43

This is true enough. So-and-so has been worked on by an expert until his small sense of grievance has grown to a large sense of grievance.

At this point, the Hook Operator directs this sense of grievance at the Powerman. If the guy-on-the-way-up is susceptible, he begins to think that the Powerman is deliberately holding him back. The Hook Operator then carefully directs the victim's attention to the Powerman's soft spot, his hidden insecurity, until the victim understands why the Powerman has this sense of inferiority and understands exactly the real inferiority which lies under this touchy sense of inferiority. This Powerman who doesn't appreciate him, the victim finally realizes, is just a dope.

When the Hook Operator gets the victim to this point, he picks up the weapon of words which he has so carefully fashioned and dangles it in front of the victim's eyes. This is what would puncture the ego of the Powerman, says, in essence, the Hook Operator. It may take days of not exactly saying this to say it exactly enough for the guy-on-the-way-up to get the point. But eventually the victim realizes that the Powerman, that unappreciative individual who thinks so little of him, can be reduced to ashes by a few words. When he has become sufficiently aggrieved and angry and has been convinced by the Hook Operator that he is well justified in feeling aggrieved and angry, the victim throws his weapon at the target. And the moment he does, he is finished, he is one less guy-on-the-way-up.

Frequently, this technique is not effective because the victim's personal morale is too high, or because his sense of balance is too good, or because he is too shrewd to be taken in by the Hook Operator. In such cases, the Hook Operator merely pretends that the guy-on-the-way-up has thrown the weapon at the Powerman's soft spot and convinces the Powerman of this.

The Hook Operator, in this case, spends his time working on the Powerman rather than on the guy-on-the-way-up. To convince the Powerman that the victim has actually thrown the weapon at the Powerman's soft spot, the Hook Operator may have to do a considerable amount of work.

44

First, he mentions a small needle of comment and claims that he heard the victim throw it at the Powerman and he follows this with another small needle. He words these little needle statements carefully so that they sound as if they just might have been said by the victim. The Hook Operator watches their effect carefully, revising the shape and length of the needles as necessary, until he notices little things which tell him that the needles are doing their work: the Powerman's tightening of the mouth when he hears them, his growing irritability with the victim, his sudden careful quiet studying of the victim.

When enough needles have been thrown and the proper effect has been achieved, the Hook Operator throws the big weapon. This may be a small knife, or a large knife, or a broadax. Once it has been thrown and it sticks and the Powerman's soft spot bleeds, the victim is done for. The guy-on-the-way-up may be an excellent and invaluable employee but so far as the Powerman is concerned, he is now only a man who threw a weapon at the soft spot the Powerman doesn't dare to look at himself, but which he can feel bleeding.

If the victim has been hooked by this second technique, he gropes and blunders about, trying to discover why the wind has suddenly changed. Occasionally a Powerman, stung into fury, lashes out at the supposed weapon-thrower and repeats what the Hook Operator has told him. But, usually, when the touchy soft spot is punctured, the Powerman cannot bring himself to do this. He cannot talk at all about the soft spot but, instead, swallows a cup of acid every time he looks at the victim. Inevitably, if the Powerman is hooked, he gets rid of the victim or he uses him as a whipping boy to console himself for his punctured ego.

It was this second technique which Gordon had used to break Ken. When Knox, outraged by the stories he heard, accused Ken of disloyalty, Ken was amazed, then annoyed, then angered. Ken was not a smooth talker and he was a man who kept hidden, under his surface impassiveness, a hundred small irritations. Within minutes two angry men were yelling at each other and nobody, anywhere, could have undone the damage. Ken, I suppose, was easy to break, and Gordon probably had little difficulty in planning exactly the right moves while he smoked his slow cigarettes.

The great difficulty with being a Hook Operator, if you have tendencies that way, is that being one is not easy. The techniques require skill, considerable acting talent, perceptivity, careful planning, a devious type of mentality, and a complete ability to rationalize your actions to yourself. The really clever Hook Operators are quite expert. They have to be. It is their livelihood. Somewhere early in the game, they became aware that they would never get anywhere with such business abilities as they possessed and they had totaled their resources and discovered that they had talents which might be substituted for the ones their jobs required, and then perfected those talents by long practice.

Of course, even the cleverest Hook Operators cannot get far if the Powermen don't have touchy ego soft spots. I suppose that the Knox organization presented a setup that was milk pudding for a Hook Operator. The Knox Company was a family organization, run by Knox Senior, an extraordinarily able and shrewd, if uneducated man, and by his six sons who were, all of them, thoroughly educated, remarkably dull, and quite aware that they wouldn't have risen higher than mail clerk in any other organization. Their awareness of their lack of ability was the main soft spot in each of the Knox boys, and the knowledge of the accumulative dullness of his six progeny was the old man's soft spot.

I remember that I was quite objective about the Hook Operators when I first learned about them, and that I looked at them coldly and clearly and thought, "They're horrible, but they're clever. It isn't easy to do what they do. It takes skill and talent and it's a pity such skill and talent can't be used constructively." It wasn't until McDermott arrived on the scene that I became afraid of the Hook Operators, and when I became afraid of them, I stopped seeing them clearly. You can do any of many things with fear and any of many things may happen to you as a result. You may run, or scream, or get ulcers. But the worst thing you can do with fear is to bury it inside of you in a box and pretend that what you're afraid of doesn't exist. When I became afraid of McDermott, that's what I did with my fear.

In the next year, Gordon moved up from the design department. A chap named Boswell moved into Gordon's job and a new man, McDermott, was hired to take over Boswell's job. The first thing I noticed about McDermott was that he spent a great deal of time at the water-cooler and out in the coffee room. I think the girls had him sized up at first as a harmless variety of wolf, but it became apparent soon enough that McDermott's interest was in gathering information about their bosses. He sounded me out instantly about Jim Knox, in whose department I worked, and I remember saying instantly that I didn't know the answer to his question. The question was harmless but I suspected it would be followed by others and I wanted to cut the conversation before it got off the ground. I tried to sound friendly and casual but I remember that McDermott's face became absolutely expressionless and that he stood looking at me for a long moment without even his eyelids blinking and then he smiled a slow, easy smile and went away and never asked me anything again. And, shortly after, I had to spend two hours talking myself out of a situation that McDermott got me into with Jim Knox.

When I first went to Knox I was told that the one thing any employee had to have, regardless of what else he had, was the confidence of the Knox family. When I first heard this comment I assumed it meant that the Knoxes had to be able to trust you with an assignment without worrying about the outcome, and also to trust you not to reveal confidential information to their competitors. I was supposed to have the confidence of Jim Knox, who supervised the department in which I worked. I suppose having Jim's confidence meant, the things I thought it meant but it also meant other things which were more important and which I didn't understand for a long time. Having Jim's confidence meant that Jim could reveal to me how little he knew about his job and be absolutely certain that I would never reveal his ignorance to anyone. It also meant, and this was even more important, that I could sit down and talk to Jim and never once reveal to him that I realized he was a bonehead who didn't have a fraction of the background he needed for his job. Also, Jim could get up from my desk after displaying how little he did know without ever having to admit to himself that he was a bonehead.

I imagine that this was easy for me to do, without even knowing that I was doing something important, because I readily accepted the fact that the Knox boys should inherit their plush jobs, sit in desks of power and draw their fantastic salaries, without feeling any resentment. Maybe this is easier for women to do than men. Women, despite their interest in making money, rarely want positions of power and importance and I have met few men who didn't want such positions and feel that they are better entitled to them than the men who have them.

McDermott was not quite so smooth as Gordon but he was far more clever. He had a brilliant mind and it was a pity that he couldn't settle for less than being a Hook Operator. But Hook Operators travel faster than ordinary men and McDermott was clearly a man in a hurry. I remember thinking in the early days, "McDermott's twisted. He can't act straight because there isn't a straight line in him." When you say this about a man like McDermott you are applying to him a standard of your own which you consider the only acceptable standard. It was my standard because it was the one by which I had been reared and conditioned and which I accepted as the only basis for human relations.

But standards are manufactured things. You don't create them; you accept them. And there are too many men like Gordon and McDermott for me to feel now that all of them are twisted. In a way, they have adapted themselves superbly to a certain type business environment. Both Gordon and McDermott cut the most direct road they could find to where they wanted to go. That they both knifed a few men getting there was totally unimportant to either of them. "Such men are immoral," people say of Hook Operators, and of course this is true. Christian principles are not the principles on which the I look Operators build their lives, although this fact, so glaringly obvious to others, is rarely apparent to the Hook Operators. I think that the strangest thing I knew about either Gordon or McDermott was that both were extremely religious men. Gordon was considered by many to be actually hipped on religion. In some fashion, such men apparently justify themselves to themselves. Maybe, if you are as clever at fooling others as Gordon and McDermott were, it's easy to be clever at fooling yourself in areas where you are eager to be fooled.

Long before Boswell took over Gordon's position in the design department, he was displaying one of the secondary talents of the Hook Operator, expert apple-polishing. He obtained the promotion because of ability, although I have no doubt that the silk-smooth apple polishing job was helpful. He hadn't been in the design department very long before it must have occurred to him that he had more brains than Gordon had; and that if. Gordon could advance to the top administrative level, he might be able to do the same thing. He hooked Gordon.

Boswell was in a choice position to do this, having inherited the mess Gordon had left. And he did it cutely, with an open-faced frankness and a somewhat bewildered air, as if he couldn't quite believe that what he was telling Leonard Knox was true. The project, went on over a period of a month. Boswell could have made his points about Gordon's inefficiency in a one-half hour conversation with Leonard; Gordon was far from being an effective organizer, and his mismanagement of the design department could clearly be proved. But Boswell brought his facts to Leonard in dribbles, carefully padding each fact with an aura that had been especially manufactured for a mind like Leonard's.

He convinced Leonard that Gordon was too clever to create such a mess just from sheer stupidity and that Gordon's purpose had been to sabotage the company. As Boswell carefully pointed out to Leonard in his guileless, "This can't be true, of course, but is there even a remote chance that it is true?" fashion, Gordon had a brother-in-law who was an executive in a company that was Knox's outstanding competitor.

The fact that the competitor was located a considerable distance away and that Gordon hadn't seen his brother-in-law in twenty years were facts which were known to Leonard, but Leonard had a "thing" about competitors stealing from Knox, and the sabotage idea took root in his mind. It was difficult for Gordon to prove that sabotage had not been in his plans and by the time he finally proved it, the stupidity that had to be stupidity because it wasn't anything else stood out crystal clear as it probably could never have stood out otherwise. Gordon was sent back to the general office and in a surprise move that stunned everyone, especially Boswell, Knox Senior moved McDermott into the design department as executive supervisor over Boswell.

That the guileless innocence used by Boswell in his approach to Leonard left him open to the criticism that he might be too guileless for an important position apparently hadn't occurred to Boswell. But it had occurred to McDermott. Two years later, Leonard revealed that McDermott had convinced him that Boswell had demonstrated that he was too innocent for his job and needed a more sophisticated man "like yourself, Leonard" to watch him. Leonard, having other things on his mind, had decided to pass the job to McDermott. The fact which struck me as oddest was that both Leonard and Jim Knox could discuss this incident and display a complete command of the facts without any understanding of the maneuvering of McDermott and Boswell.

Maybe it takes a certain type mentality even to recognize the Hook Operators. I know that none of the Knoxes showed any understanding of them, but: that, Carmody, the sales manager, understood them very well, and that young Sam Jackson, the office boy, saw them sharply in focus and had them pegged neatly and accurately in their individual holes. Maybe you have to he reared in a certain type environment or be conditioned over a period or maybe you need a certain type mind to see the Hook Operators clearly, I remember thinking, the day that McDermott was promoted again, this time to the top administrative level as Leonard Knox's personal advisor, that there wasn't any way to cope with men like McDermott and feeling afraid, and also relieved that I wasn't in McDermott's way. I was quite afraid of McDermott by that time. The day that McDermott hooked Carmody was the day that my feeling of relief vanished and I was left with fear.

Carmody had been with Knox for twenty years. He was extremely capable in his job as sales manager and he had helped greatly to build the Knox organization to the position it had. We had been hearing that McDermott was needling Carmody constantly in the brass meetings. Carmody had a temper and a sharp decisive way of talking, and an iron-hand, no-interference-from-you-Knoxes policy in his department that displayed clearly the contempt he had for the Knox family, He had retained the confidence of the Knoxes for twenty years, despite his tactless handling of them, for a reason that was so important: it outweighed all other considerations. He made tons of money for the Knox family.

I suppose Knox Senior had always resented the feeling that Carmody gave him of being a busybodying dope, and resented even more the fact that, he had to smile while he took it on the jaw. I still don't think old man Knox would have turned on Carmody unless he had been persuaded first that Carmody was no longer indispensable. When Jim Knox said something one afternoon to the effect that McDermott was developing a great respect for the talents of Sorey Sanderson, Carmody's top assistant, I sensed that McDermott was after Carmody's scalp. Sorey was no particular friend of McDermott's but: neither was he an enemy, as Carmody obviously was. And in McDermott's mind, there was not an inch of space for an individual whom he saw as an enemy.

McDermott suddenly started to promote a sales campaign that he was certain Carmody wouldn't tolerate inasmuch as it violated Carmody's pet ideas about sales programs. The argument between Carmody and McDermott went on until Carmody flew into a temper one day, stated flatly that he would resign before he would put McDermott's ideas into effect, and said a few dozen things about the asininity of old man Knox for even contemplating such a program. A month later Sorey took over the sales department and Carmody left the organization.

By this time I had been with Knox for seven years, was making an excellent salary and had a clear opportunity to receive an even more excellent salary within a short time. These are the things with which you hook yourself. I was hooked sufficiently to tell my-self that if I walked out of Knox I would only walk into another firm where a similar situation existed. I think I was fairly right in assuming this but it was still stupid of me to stay. By that time I had built up a fear toward an environment which I saw clearly and understood very well. I had explored every groove to find an escape from the fear I was building and couldn't find it. Had I gone to an-other firm I would have had a change of scene and an opportunity to escape from the terror that wrapped itself around me every morning that I walked into Knox. But I had a great deal at Knox and I wanted to hold onto it.

I worried over McDermott so much that finally I had to erase him from my mind and pretend that he wasn't what he was and that the things that were happening weren't happening. When you reach that stage with fear, you start growing strange plants of distortion in your mind. The best comparison I can think of to illustrate this mental process occurs in George Orwell's 1984. An entire staff of government employees spend their time rewriting the files of old newspapers and documents, changing hurts so that the facts agree with whatever propaganda program the government has in progress. You do this to yourself mentally when you set about deliberately distorting a picture you can see clearly. By the time you have twisted the facts to agree with the picture you wish to see, your subconscious mind has helpfully plodded through the past and distorted a lifetime of facts to make them agree with your present self-deception program.

I suppose that I had a certain degree of security from having Jim Knox's confidence and that this factor would have kept me stabilized for a long time. I never did lose Jim's confidence except that all the things that Jim stood for in the way of security to me disappeared overnight. Not McDermott, but another man, Litter, did a job on Jim. Litter used the youngest of the Knox boys to hook Jim and I know that I was shaken out of my dull avoidance of what was going on by the realization that even the Knoxes were willing to hatchet each other.

The youngest Knox was the dullest of the lot and had the

least chance of getting into a plush job even in his father's organization. Maybe that helped him to see things Litter's way. When the earthquake was over, Jim was working in a field job and the youngest Knox was supervising Jim's department with Litter as his assistant. And all the sense of security I had in my relations to the Knox family was gone. I was left in a room with Litter's shark eyes making holes in me and a cold chill in my spine.

A short time later, I left Knox. I didn't leave it in a way I could possibly ever have anticipated. I never blamed anybody for the months that were to follow except myself. Litter might have done a job on me in time but he didn't get the chance. I walked out of Knox with a hook in my back that was entirely of my own making. When I finally pulled it out and had a good look at it, I decided that nobody could have stuck it in my back except myself, and the only satisfaction I got was that I was able to pull it out myself, and see clearly the shape of it.

*Part Two*

# The Operators

When I awoke they were standing at the foot of my bed looking like soft fuzzy ghosts. I tried feeling the bedclothes. The sensation of feeling was sharp. I was awake and this was real.

The boy was about twelve years old, handsome, and with a pleasant, relaxed smile. The elderly man was impressive: solid, conservative, a reliable man with built-in rules. The third was a real weirdo with hair three inches too long, black, straight, and limp, and with a body that was also long and limp. The face didn't belong with the body or the hair; the features were fine and sensitive, the expression, arrogant and unbending.

The elderly man suddenly cleared his throat. "It is necessary for the good of all concerned that you get to know Hinton better." He turned and looked at the weirdo.

I was positive that I had never seen that face before. The elderly man apparently sensed my thoughts. "You know him well," he said; "you used to know him better."

I said hurriedly, "If you say so, we must have met. I'm sorry I can't recall Mr. Hinton." To the arrogant face I said, "How are you?" Hinton bowed his head a quarter of an inch and stared stiffly out the window.

"I am Burt," said the elderly man. He seemed concerned but in a dead, resigned sort of way, a man who had lived long with order and system and who was having difficulty adjusting to the role of master of ceremonies at a holocaust.

"And this is Nicky." The boy smiled a wide, sunny smile.

Burt explained. I could see why he had been chosen spokesman. What he had to say, he said clearly and in a few words. I had been selected for participation in an experiment. He hoped I would be co-operative; lack of cooperation on my part would make matters difficult for them and for myself. They were Operators, the three of them. There were Operators everywhere in the world although they rarely were seen or heard. My seeing and hearing them was, unfortunately, a necessary part of the experiment.

I thought: I have come upon knowledge which other people do not have and the knowledge is obviously dangerous to have; others would be in equal danger if I revealed it to them.

"Yes," said Burt, and he looked pleased.

But I hadn't spoken. I considered this for a moment. First things first, "What is the nature of this experiment?"

Hinton smiled wryly. "Didn't I tell you," he said to Burt, "that it would say that first?"

It?

Burt continued. A great Operator whose name was Hadley had wanted to make an experiment of this type for some time. The experiment consisted of selecting a person like myself, revealing the facts of the Operators' world to the individual, and observing the results.

A guinea pig in a cage, I thought. So much for that. Second things second. Could they or couldn't they? Yes, there wasn't much doubt about it. They were reading my mind. I could see it in the way their eyes focused on my face, the expressions on their faces, as they watched me think.

Burt explained: Every thought in the mind of a person like myself was always clear to any Operator who might be tuned in.

I considered this situation. Would I, perhaps, be able to think on some sub-cellar level and so reduce this tremendous advantage they had?

Nicky grinned broadly and Burt smiled gently. Burt again: No thought of my mind on any level could escape them. Operators could penetrate the minds of Things at any level.

Things!

Hinton sighed. "Things. Yes, of course. Think of the word with a capital initial, if you like. It may help your ego a bit. All people like you are Things to us—Things whose minds can be read and whose thoughts can be initiated and whose actions can be motivated. Does that surprise you? It goes on all the time. There is some, but far less, free will than you imagine. A Thing does what some Operator wants it to do, only it remains under the impression that its thoughts originate in its own mind. Actually, you have more free will at this moment than most of your kind ever have. For you at least know that what we are saying is coming from us, not from you."

It!

"There's nothing wrong with its will," Burt said.

Hinton looked at him intently. "We're dropping you," he said.

"I'm going to stick," Burt said. He turned and looked at Nicky.

Nicky seemed distressed. "There's something you must know," Nicky said, turning to me. "All Things are operated at all times, by some Operator. In recent years, Burt operated you."

Could be, I thought. That would explain the even flow, the sanity, of recent years. Burt was a sane man, logical, judicious, unexcitable.

"Before Burt," Nicky continued, "it was Hinton."

Hinton? Incredible!

There was a stir in the air and a new shape appeared in the room.

"It's Sharp," said Nicky. "Hadley's representative," he told Hinton. Hinton grunted.

Sharp looked like an amiable little ferret. To be watched carefully, I thought. Sharp looked at me sharply. "Interesting," he said, and moved closer.

Behind the far wall a discordant hum, like static, rose and filled the apartment.

"Interference," Burt said. "I expected it."

Sharp looked grim. "I didn't think this would be easy. Do you realize that we may get life jeopardy if we're caught? That's an outside Operator. Block him off."

Hinton appeared to be concentrating on the rhythm of the sounds. "At least a dozen of them," he said. "I imagine it's the city council."

The sharp static mellowed into speech and the voices of the city council Operators, protesting vehemently at Hadley's experiment, flooded the apartment. I hoped that some of the protests might show concern for my welfare, but the protest was narrow in scope and clearly defined. Information which no Thing should ever have was being divulged to a Thing; the Thing might give the information to other Things, thereby creating a hazardous situation.

"I assure you," Sharp said loudly, "that this Thing is very close mouthed." To Hinton he whispered, "I thought you bought these guys off."

Hinton shook his head. "I was working on a deal to get out of the city fast."

"Jeopardy," said one of the council voices. "Life-long jeopardy."

A dozen voices began to talk at once. In the bedlam, Nicky came closer and sat on the edge of the bed. "What you must understand," he said to me, "is that jeopardy is a jail sentence for an Operator. When an Operator is in jeopardy, he can't operate at all." He sounded as if he expected me to understand and, in some way, help.

"What is a city council?" I asked him.

"The highest legal authority for Operators in any city. They'll try to stop this experiment. And it must go on."

So the Operators were subject to law and authority as were Things. Was this better for me, or worse? I listened to the bedlam for a while, remembered suddenly that I had a piece of work, nine-tenths finished, in my office, rose, dressed, and went out. Hinton and Nicky were still with me when I reached the street.

Concentrating was difficult but I managed to finish the work on my desk. Hinton and Nicky talked constantly, and occasionally I looked up to see one of their grey shapes floating down the middle of the office. At noon I turned the work over to a clerk, gave her directions for mailing it, told the manager that I was ill, and went home.

The council Operators had gone but Burt and Sharp were still in the apartment. I listened carefully when Hinton discussed my fellow employees in the office. He appeared to be identifying them individually as Operators or Things. I thought a loud question.

"Yes," Burt said. "Operators move about in the flesh. So far as surface appearance is concerned, Operators are identical with Things. No Thing would be able to distinguish one from the other, but Operators can distinguish them easily. An Operator need only extend and contact the individual's mind and he knows instantly whether he's tuned in on an Operator or a Thing."

I scrutinized their soft, grey, fuzzy, shapes. "Sure, we have bodies," Nicky said. "What you're looking at now are pictures of ourselves that we're projecting."

And where were the bodies?

"Close by." Nicky grinned. "Don't come looking for us, though. "We'd blank you out before you could reach us."

"Indoctrination," said Sharp, looking at his fingernails.

Burt cleared his throat. "The one great difference between an Operator and a Thing is the construction and ability of the mind.

Operators are born with special brain cells known as the battlement. With these cells, an Operator can extend and probe into the mind of a Thing. He can tap the Thing's mind and discover what is going on there, and even feed thoughts to the Thing's mind in order to motivate it. The mental difference is one of ability, not one of quality. Operators, like Things, may be stupid or intelligent. But that one difference permits the Operators to rule the Things."

I was dumbfounded. Why had Things never become aware of all this?

"There are some Things engaged in research along those lines," Nicky said. "But I really doubt that it will make much difference if Things ever do discover that they're ruled by Operators. They're far too conceited ever to believe it."

I was on my second cup of coffee when the council Operators returned. Their voices shaking with indignation, they handed down an ultimatum. Sharp and company had two hours to clear out. As soon as they had gone, a council Operator would take me over.

In the silence that followed the council's departure, the grey faces of Hinton and Sharp turned and looked at me steadily. Whether I knew it or not, Sharp said, I was in more danger from the council than I was from them. The moment they walked out, the council would return and destroy me.

"That's cloak-and-dagger stuff," I told him.

Hinton sighed. "At least, buy some nails and a hammer and nail down the windows. Because that's the way you're going to go. Wait until you have twenty Operators from the council in here, working on your mind, telling you to jump. Believe me, you'll jump. So far as the council is concerned, you're a monstrosity and a source of danger, something that has to be put out of the way."

I evaluated the shock, horror, and anger in the voices of the council Operators, packed an overnight bag, went down to the bus depot, and bought a ticket for the nearest large city.

"We'll be in touch with you," Sharp told me. "We'll be in a car, following."

I wondered: Would another city have a council of Operators who would interfere and would the interference be to my advantage?

"There are city councils everywhere," Nicky said suddenly. "There are Operators everywhere. There isn't a section of the country where Things aren't controlled by Operators. You can't escape them if that's what you're hoping for. Besides, Hadley has your charter."

What was a charter?

"The right to operate a Thing. Hadley purchased it from your company. And until he sells it to someone else, you can depend upon it, this experiment will continue. And, believe me, if any council confiscates the charter, the first thing they'll do is to destroy you."

There had to be some way, some way.

"Do you know how much chance you've got of getting out of this?" Nicky said. "One in three hundred. And you'll have to be lucky."

I brooded and listened to Hinton and Sharp talking. Their car couldn't be too far away because their voices were coming in clear and loud. Sleeping and eating were impossible. When the bus slid into the depot, finally, and I got off, my legs wobbled.

"Quickly," Sharp said. "Take out all personal identification and destroy it. I don't have time to explain. There's great danger."

Social security card. Wallet card. I tore them into small pieces and threw them into a trash can and waited. While I was waiting, the floor of the depot slanted upward.

"Looks like a heart attack," said a voice over my head. After a time, somebody in a white jacket was pressing something against my chest. Then I was in an ambulance. While I was in the ambulance, it turned into a hospital ward. I was walking through clouds of fog, talking and talking. A nurse, bending over me, called someone and a tight little crowd of heads bent over me and listened and asked questions and listened. Then I was led carefully onto and off an elevator and into a strange looking car. A policeman sat in the back with me. We arrived at a building and the policeman assisted me inside. A woman took me over, led me into a small office and after a while I learned where I was. A psychiatric ward.

The fog fell away and I was suddenly alert. Damn Sharp, I thought. It didn't take him long. He's got me where I can't escape.

I tried to answer the woman's questions sensibly, found concentrating difficult. I had been too long without sleep and food. Who was the President of the United States? I couldn't recall. What year was it? Nineteen-fifty-something. Where was my home? Sharp's voice came to my rescue.

"Los Angeles."

"Los Angeles," I repeated. I was certain that I didn't live in Los Angeles but where did I live? An attendant appeared, took away my possessions, gave me a cotton robe and a pair of carpet slippers, and led me to a ward. My eyes seemed to be working independently of my mind, taking a quick inventory. The number of beds in the ward, the number of bodies in the beds, the number and texture of the attendants, the location of the windows. My eyes, not my mind, noted the hypodermic needle in the hands of the attendant who came toward me.

Sharp hissed, "Don't let them give it to you. There's great danger."

I objected to the hypodermic. The attendant gave me a blank look, went away, and came back with another attendant, a female wrestler.

I repeated my objection to the hypodermic. Something flared out of the eyes of the wrestler. Hate, sharp and clear, not mistakable for irritation or annoyance.

My tongue went into action. Like my eyes, it seemed to be working independently. I heard myself talking softly, smoothly, rationally. My physical condition, I said, made it inadvisable for me to take sedatives. My physician had warned me of this many times. If the injection was a sedative, there might be a physical reaction. It would be wise, therefore, to consult a doctor before giving it to me.

The first attendant looked at me blankly and shrugged her shoulders. Defeat was unimportant. The wrestler pressed her lips together and glared. Defeat was not unimportant. The first attendant eased away. The wrestler glared, glared, glared, finally departed.

After they had gone I wondered briefly why I had said what I had said. So far as I knew, I had no physical condition which would prevent my taking a sedative. I consulted my watch. Two-thirty in the morning. The voices of Sharp, Hinton and Nicky returned. News had come to them from my home town. The council was furious that I was still alive. One of the council Operators was coming to the city. His purpose: to kill me. He'd have a fat chance of getting into the women's ward of the hospital I was in, I decided.

"He really could do it with rays from outside of the building," Nicky told me. "We'll try to keep him off until we can get you out of here. I hope we can."

So did I. I stayed awake through the night wondering if they would. By morning, I was still waiting.

The bodies on the beds turned out to be an assortment of girls. They congregated in the corridor, smoking, getting lights from each other's cigarettes. I was surprised to find my own cigarettes in the pocket of my robe. The matches had been confiscated. The girls moved suddenly down to the long tables at the end of the floor and I followed them. Breakfast. I skipped food, drank as many cups of coffee as I could get. I approached a girl who was sitting on a bench smoking, asked if I might light my cigarette from hers. She looked up at me, burst into tears, bowed her head and sobbed and sobbed. I remembered suddenly where I was. A mental case, poor girl. I got a light from someone else and came back to the ward to find the beds made and an attendant standing before them defiantly. I went looking for a seat but the benches were filled. Would I have to stand up all day?

The light faded and the floor came up slowly and gently. Big hands grabbed my ankles and shoulders, and I was heaved onto a bed, face down. I turned my head so I could breathe and fell asleep.

"Lunch," Sharp was hissing in my ear. "You need some strength. Eat everything."

How did Sharp know it was lunchtime? I looked vaguely down the floor. The girls were moving toward the tables again and I followed. No knives. No forks. I ate everything I could get my soup spoon around, came back, lay on the bed again, fell asleep again.

I never dreamed so they couldn't be dreams. "They're not," Nicky said clearly. "They're black-out movies." Portraits of the Operators, in full color, rose before my eyes. I thought the picture of Burt was malicious; he had been painted with horns on his head. Each portrait hung in front of my eyes for a few moments; then, an invisible hand holding a visible black crayon crossed out the portrait with a huge X. Looking at the portraits, I fell asleep.

I awoke alert and curiously aware that something was about to happen. I watched the girls but they were making no movement toward the tables. I sat on the side of the bed and waited and the door flew open and a nurse came in, a card in her hand. She walked to the center of the ward and bawled out my name and I rose and followed her downstairs. The sleep had refreshed me. I entered the office she pointed to, said "How do you do," to the doctor, and sat down. The shapes of Hinton, Sharp, and Nicky shot up suddenly behind the doctor's shoulders. I ignored them and kept my eyes on the doctor's face.

He had a sheaf of forms on his desk and his job, apparently, was to fill them out.

Sharp and Hinton were arguing. Curiously, both were in favor of erasing all information about Operators from my mind. Hinton believed that the blotting out process could best be achieved by blackout movies. Sharp agreed with this. He was in favor of my staying in the hospital to have the movies administered. Hinton objected. So did Nicky.

The doctor asked me a question and Sharp threw the answer at me. I repeated and the doctor wrote it down.

"Its family would hear about its being here and they'd worry," Nicky said.

"Exactly," Hinton said. "The picture is complicated enough without a bunch of relatives on our necks. The blackout movies can be arranged anywhere. The important thing is to get out of here fast."

The doctor asked me another question. Sharp gave me the answer. I repeated it.

Sharp thought that the blackout movie apparatus in the hospital was excellent. Hinton disagreed. The doctor reviewed my medical history at long length. Sharp gave me the answers. The doctor finished filling out the forms and examined me. He tapped my knees, scraped the soles of my feet, tested my balance, took my blood pressure, examined my heart. Sharp was objecting less about leaving.

The doctor wanted to know about my family. With Sharp's assistance, I manufactured an assortment of people and invented addresses for them. We discussed my fainting spell in the depot. Sharp gave in and agreed to leaving.

The doctor wrote something on a card and told me to give it to the nurse in my ward. I did, collected my clothes, dressed, and walked out. Hinton, still worrying about the council, advised me to get to another bus depot immediately.

It hadn't been so difficult escaping, I thought. But it was obvious that without Sharp my escape could never have been achieved.

"GREYHOUND IS CONTROLLED BY OPERATORS," NICKY
TOLD ME, "AND THEY POLICE THEIR BUSES."

# Greyhound

I learned that the Greyhound Bus Company was a favorite vehicle of transport for Operators.

"Greyhound is controlled by Operators," Nicky told me, "and they police their buses. None of the airlines or railroads do and their carriers are in an outlaw state. You never know when some Operator is going to molest the Thing in your custody. The driver of a Greyhound bus is always an Operator, licensed as an Operator cop, a Shield. If you have a Thing with you, you post the Thing's charter with the driver and he sees to it that no other Operator disturbs it."

Sharp complained suddenly that the bus was filled with flies. "And I'm not referring to flies," Sharp told me. "I'm referring to Flies."

"Fly is slang for an Operator who doesn't belong to an organization as we do," Nicky explained. "Flies can be a nuisance and sometimes they can be dangerous if they try to molest your Thing. But I don't think we have to worry on a Greyhound bus."

"Listen," said a strange voice.

"It's the driver," said Sharp.

"I don't like this business," said the driver. "That's risky, having a Thing sit there taking in everything you're saying. I don't think my company would care to go along with that kind of business."

Sharp explained about the experiment.

"You're walking on eggshells," the driver told him. "What you ought to do is get a bill of resuscitation."

I could feel Sharp's ears picking up. "A bill of resuscitation,"

Sharp said, licking each word. "That's an idea."

"Ingenious," said Nicky.

"I think so. Nicky, you stay in. Hinton and I are going to have a private word with the driver."

"Bills of resuscitation are issued when Things need to be revived," Nicky told me. "A Thing has to be pretty far gone before an Operator can get a bill issued, but Sharp may be able to manage it. With a bill like that in his pocket, Sharp would be safe with most city councils. He'd be able to justify the experiment as necessary to revive a dead Thing."

Sharp came back. "The driver is going to wire his office at the next stop. He thinks we'll get the bill. It's a wonderful break for us. Operating under the bill's authority, we'll be able to get to California without interference."

Apparently Hadley's organization was in California and the boys were getting me there as fast as they could. Obviously, California was the most dangerous place I could go. When Sharp announced late that night that the bill of resuscitation had been issued, I made my decision. When we arrived in Chicago, despite all Sharp's protests, I headed south for New Orleans—on a train.

The Flies on the train tuned in, cut off Sharp, Hinton and Nicky and immediately began to play The Game. The first step in The Game was the selection of the subject around which The Game would revolve. A large board appeared in front of my eyes with a list of items printed on it. The first item, I noticed, was Sudden Death.

"Skip that," said one of the Flies. "Let's stick to the subject this Thing is concerned with. You may get highly artificial responses, otherwise. This is a Thing that is forced to listen to Operators. Let's take Operators as the subject."

One of the Flies was appointed adjudicator and The Game began. The first Fly talked to me. Did I realize that for the rest of my life I would be living this kind of existence—that I would never again live the normal life of a Thing? For the rest of my days, I would be forced to sit and listen to the Operators talk. I would have, not life, but Operators' conversations.

The idea struck me like a blow. I could feel my heart jump.

"Are you heating it up?" asked the adjudicator, who seemed to exercise the duties of scorekeeper and referee.

"Yes," said the first Fly, "isn't it permitted?"

"There's some heart action," said the adjudicator. "Decrease the heat ten points and don't go above that."

"I'm through, anyway," said the Fly. "I got my reaction."

The second Fly came in. Did I have any idea what would happen to me when I reached Hadley? Had I seen or heard of animals in experimental laboratories, cut and tortured while conscious, so that some doctor could observe and learn? This would be the same thing except that I would be the animal.

"It's the same thing right now," I shot back at him. "That's what you're doing."

"You didn't get very far," said the adjudicator. "You're out."

The third Fly came in. Did I know that Hadley had a cage full of freaks in his laboratory, an entire block full of Things upon which he experimented? Hadley was famous from coast to coast for his experiments. There was a woman who had been convinced that she was an apostle of the sun and who thought she dined every night with the sun god. She had used her delusions to start a new religion among Things and had made quite a bit of money out of it. I might make money out of what lay ahead of me, too, but I might have to look at gorillas crawling around my room day and night.

My skin was tingling. The Mad Scientist, I thought suddenly, and laughed. The Fly grunted and departed.

The Game came to its close finally. The adjudicator announced the winner and the winning Fly scooped up the pot of "points" to which each Fly had contributed. The Game was clear enough. Each Fly had dripped his drop of poison, obtained an emotional reaction from me. The one who had aroused in me the greatest fear, I noticed, was the one who had won.

"It's not usually done this way," one of the Flies told me while the points were being put up for a new pot. "Ordinarily, the Thing can't hear us, although he gets the ideas we inject, anyway. But your mind is wide open, which is why you can hear us talk."

The Game continued. I tried to build up an emotional rigor against the impact of what I heard but it was hours before I managed to achieve even a surface impassiveness. The Game went on and on through the night. By the time the train reached New Orleans, I was ready to throw myself into a river. Hinton, Sharp, and Nicky caught up with me in the baggage room.

"For your sake and for ours," Hinton advised me, "stick to buses."

"Its heart is going like fury," said Nicky. "Let's get to a hotel, fast."

At the hotel I got my clothes off and fell into bed. "Pour sedation in," said Sharp. "It'll have to be knocked out for hours." I fell asleep and awoke seventeen hours later. I had intended staying in New Orleans for a time, but rain was falling dismally, the city was chilly and damp, and I had developed a racking cough. I decided to get into sunnier country. Via a Greyhound bus.

I bought a ticket to a town in Texas and tried to plan my escape. I would have to get away from the boys, somehow, and hope that somewhere I would find an Operator who would close my mind.

IF I COULD GET A TWO-BLOCK DISTANCE FROM
ALL OPERATORS, I THOUGHT, MY MIND WOULD HAVE
PEACE AND MIGHT HEAL AND CLOSE.

"Are you tuned in on this Thing," Nicky asked Sharp and Hinton. "We're taking good care of you," he told me reproachfully.

"You don't realize it."

"Gorillas," said Hinton and grunted.

"We just drained your head," Nicky told me. "We wanted to find out what those Flies had been talking about. In draining, we get a full account of everything you've heard, thought and seen. Those Flies were a pack of dogs."

A thought occurred to me. "Over what distance can an Operator influence the mind of a Thing?"

"About two and a half city blocks. Not all Operators can extend that far, though. Some of them can't extend beyond twenty feet. It depends upon the size and quality of the individual Operator's battlement."

If I could get a two-block distance from all Operators, I thought, my mind would have peace and might heal and close. Obviously, the Operators had opened my mind wide so that any Operator could tune in. What I needed to carry out my plan was money. If I went home, I could draw out what money I had in the bank and buy a small house with a lot of land around it. And without Operators to influence me, my mind might close in time. Also, I thought, without Operators to influence me, I might discover what I was really like. I could see why I might have been two very different people during the years Hinton and Burt had operated me. People lived out their lifetimes, I reflected, taking strange actions, never aware that their actions were motivated by some Operator. The Game, as it had been played on the train, was a horrible kind of sport but apparently in the relationship between Operators and Things, there were even more vicious elements than The Game. Things could be motivated into horrible actions for heartless reasons.

"Sure," Nicky said suddenly. "I knew an Operator who put a gun in his Thing's hand and sent it out to kill some Operator he hated. Of course, stuff like that you can't get away with. The Operator got life jeopardy and could never operate again."

Such laws as Operators were subject to had obviously been

made to protect Operators. Nowhere was there compassion or sense of responsibility for Things,

"Are you shocked because Things are exploited?" Nicky wanted to know. "Doesn't your own kind exploit every form of life it can exploit ? There's nothing more ruthless than a Thing. Your kind is in no position to criticize."

"I should think," I told him, "that Operators would feel toward Things at least the way that Things feel toward dogs."

"That's about it," said Nicky.

"But that's not it. Apparently nature developed two species of men. One could help and benefit the other. Instead, one exploits the other without compassion."

Sharp got into the conversation. "What you're overlooking is that a Thing can be influenced chiefly because of its desire for money and power. An Operator's security and self-esteem revolve about Operator's points just as a Thing's revolves about money. With sufficient points, an Operator can do anything in an Operator's world. He can be a great power. He can own an organization and buy the charters of hundreds of Things. He can be safe from other Operators. How does that make him more despicable than a Thing? The hell of it is, Operators and Things are motivated by similar desires. We're both in the soup, Operators and Things alike."

If I could rent a little house somewhere, with a great deal of land about it, I speculated, I might be able to get beyond reach of the Operators. I returned to my home town, drew out the money I had in the bank and, despite the boys' glum prophecies, took a bus north.

In a sparsely inhabited section of a sparsely inhabited state, I went looking for a cabin. A real estate agent immediately brought me to a mountain cabin, told me how wonderful mountain air was, and left me there.

"Indians," Hinton said, after I had taken a walk around. "My God, actual Indians." The boys, I discovered to my disappointment, were still with me. I wondered where they were and decided that they had managed to find refuge in one of the little shacks that surrounded my cottage and which were inhabited by Spanish-speaking Mexican-Indian families. My cabin, I had discovered, was not nearly so isolated as it had appeared to be. Besides the little shacks which were completely hidden among trees, there were a dozen or so large size cabins close by, one of them a stone's throw from my own.

I took long daily walks, hoping to get beyond the range of the boys' voices but the voices trailed after me wherever I went.

"Sharp is using stroboscope," Nicky told me, finally. "We can extend for a mile with it."

I walked daily to the combination post office, grocery and variety store that lay about a mile north of my cabin to buy groceries and to chat with the postmaster's family.

"Wonderful fresh air up here," Nicky said. "I might gain some weight. A really healthful place to live."

But Hinton and Sharp battled at me constantly to move on. "Indians," Hinton kept saying, "actual Indians."

I had been in the cabin about a month when I decided, prompted by the postmaster, to walk the three miles to the highway and to take the bus to town. "I make the trip once a month, myself," the postmaster (who, I afterward remembered, usually traveled with a gun) told me. "I realize how lucky I am to be up in the mountains every time I get back."

I arrived in town early one afternoon, walked around, arrived back at the bus station to discover that the bus I had planned to take had been "discontinued for a couple of days," and that I would have to wait three hours for the next one. I went for a walk and Hinton urged me to go into a drug store and buy a flashlight, a request that seemed absurd, but I finally made the purchase.

By the time the next bus had deposited me at my stop in the mountains, I understood Hinton's desire for the flashlight. Night had fallen and the three-mile hike before me was over a road almost hidden in the trees. I snapped on the flash and started walking, listening to the boys chat, and listening also to the little sounds that came out of the forest: chirps, grunts, yips, slight scurryings, the crack of twigs breaking.

I was almost home and could see my cabin down at the bottom of the road just beyond another cabin which housed a Spanish-speaking man and his wife and which was fronted by a spacious yard in which lived seven yappy dogs. The boys were discussing Indians and the possible exploitation of them by Operators at some time in the future, when Nicky suddenly materialized beside me, his pleasant face smiling. It had been a good while since I had seen any of the Operators and I was somewhat surprised.

"Quick," Nicky said. "Shine your flash down on the dogs."

If it had been Sharp or Hinton, I might have argued. Because it was pleasant, kind Nicky, I raised my flash and waved it about until the light fell on the dogs. They exploded in shrill, yappy barks.

"Now, quickly," said Nicky, "turn around and shine it back on the road." I did and something as big as a Great Dane was on the road, not too far behind me, its eyes shining with a peculiar metallic light.

"Shine it right in his face and move it up and down." I jiggled the flash and the light went up and down over the shining eyes. The eyes were turned off suddenly and something that looked as big as the back of a bull went into the forest.

"On the dogs again," said Nicky, "and run."

I went down the road, running like a jackrabbit, my flash on the dogs. The dogs, yelping fiercely, were trying to tear down the fence. Before I reached them, the Spanish-speaking man had come out into the yard and was speaking Spanish like an express train.

I stopped running, got my breath, and said, "I'm terribly sorry." The Spanish-speaking man waved his head from side to side and the dogs yelped and yelped. I went back to my cabin, thinking of the yellow eyes. Nicky suddenly reminded me that I wanted to pick some of the little white flowers that grew outside the cabin. I picked some and brought them indoors and put them in water and listened to Nicky talk about flowers and after a while I forgot the yellow eyes and went to bed.

The next morning Sharp announced that it was absolutely imperative that we move on and this time Nicky agreed with him, pointing out to me that the water supply was inadequate and I could take only one bath a week and would probably have germs all over me shortly. Hinton pointed out wryly that if my purpose in staying in the mountains was to escape them, it was obvious that I wasn't going to succeed.

I agreed that there didn't seem to be much point in my staying, and the next morning I had a neighbor drive me into town.

At breakfast the next morning Nicky said that he had received a communication from my ex-company complaining that I was a top-grade horse that was being ruined.

"A Thing is used by companies as a horse or a bronco, depending upon its temperament," Nicky explained to me. "Horses are Things who stew and worry but never do anything to resolve their problems. Horses are wonderful for The Game. Broncos are a different type, entirely. They never sit around brooding. When trouble comes, they kick up their heels, plunge right in, and settle the business one way or another. You were a bronco before Burt got hold of you. Burt changed you to a horse. This experiment isn't exactly being conducted for your benefit, but one benefit you'll get from it is that it will change you back to a bronco."

I was musing over this when the boys got into a discussion about Flies. "You're going to have trouble with them constantly," Sharp said. "Even on buses. The thing to do is to get to California quick."

"We might go by way of Canada," Nicky suggested. "I don't think they permit Flies too much liberty up there."

"A very intelligent suggestion," Hinton said wryly, "especially as we don't have licenses to operate in Canada."

It was enough for me. I made for a telephone booth, called the airport, and determined when the next plane left for Canada.

"Oh, God," said Hinton.

"Well," Sharp said, "you were the one who claimed this Thing had gotten info a rut. It's taking three of us just to keep up with it."

A few hours later, unaccompanied by the boys, I was on a plane bound for Canada. Had it really happened? Had I shaken them off?

"Its head is wide open," said a voice. "There isn't an inch of protection of any kind on its head. No shack, no board, no cover. Also, it seems to be aware of everything we're saying."

"Its head is open," said another voice, "and it's on the loose. I'm picking it up. One of the disadvantages in being a Drawfly is that you always need drawbait."

"Pick it up when it gets off the plane," said Operator One. "Are you sure it has information about Operators?"

"I've been draining it like mad," said Operator Two. "Its head is loaded with information about Operators. Where in hell did it ever get such data?"

"I'm operating it for the time being," said Operator One. His voice rose. "Ladies and gentlemen, I have with me one of the queerest Things you've ever seen. It knows about Operators."

"Dear God," said a woman's voice, "who owns it?"

"We're operating it for the time being. Any of you may come in and explore for fifteen points. You can probe and drain, but you can't work." A dozen or so voices came in, one by one, paid their points, asked me questions, all of which I ignored.

"Now," said Operator Two, "who wants to play The Game? Twenty points for the play."

The Operators were lining up for The Game when the stewardess announced suddenly that the plane would land shortly. The Drawfly sighed. "At any rate," he said, "we made two hundred points. Not bad. This Thing is a gold mine. I'm going to stick to its heels."

But at the airport I got into a cab, went to a bus depot, and escaped. I headed for a northern city in Canada, was taken over immediately by a Canadian Drawfly who, shortly afterward, sold me to another Drawfly. When I had a chance to change buses again, I headed back to the United States and immediately fell into the net of the vicious Dorraine.

"He's a good guy in some ways," the woman told me, "but he hates Things. I'll do what I can for you but that won't be much. If you get a chance, make a break for it."

His name was Dorraine and the woman was his wife. As soon as they came into my life, my head began to ache fiercely. I settled down into the bus seat and gritted my teeth, but my quiet fortitude disappeared in a spasm of fright when I learned that the pain was caused by Dorraine.

"He's trying to destroy the brain cells you use in reasoning," his wife told me. To her husband she cried, "Stop it, for God's sake. You've got a quarter-inch chiseled off the left side already. If you keep it up, you'll finish with an imbecile."

Not if I could help it. At the first stop I got off the bus and made for a hotel.

"Get into bed and call a doctor," Mrs. Dorraine advised. "And don't waste time. Chiseling is dangerous."

I selected a doctor's name from the phone book, called him, and went to bed. The doctor arrived, examined me and ordered me to a hospital immediately. "I'll take you in my car," he told me.

"What has happened to my head?"

"Your head?" He looked at me oddly. "You have pneumonia. I'll wait for you downstairs."

An hour later, I was hospitalized. I slept for long periods, awoke to hear the Dorraines scrapping with each other, and fell asleep listening to them. Either they were in a nearby hotel, I decided, or were parked in a car outside the hospital.

A week later I was considerably improved and I realized, as I mused over my state of affairs that the Operators' Game could be of benefit to me. The Dorraines had been trying to recruit players among the patients. Among the patients I had already found Operators who disliked the Dorraines enough to want to get me away from them.

"You're loose," said one of the Operators who identified himself as a man recuperating from an appendectomy. "There are certain rules which can be enforced with loose Things in this state. Whoever wins a loose Thing in The Game obtains the Thing for a period of twenty-four hours. We're going to try to win you and if we do, we'll give you a rest."

As the winner in The Game was the Operator who could get the greatest emotional reaction from the Thing, the terrorizing Dorraine could have won me easily every time. However, by controlling my own reactions, I was in a good position to determine the winner of each game. To Dorraine's deep disgust, other Operators won me day after day. A pair of kitchen workers won me and urged me to write letters to my friends.

"We'll help you phrase them," one of the women said. "If your friends are Operators, they'll be able to decode the letters and learn what's really happening to you."

I wrote the letters just as the Operators dictated them and although I scanned them closely for indications of a code, I could find none. The letters seemed to be no more than cheerful accounts of the places I had seen and the good times I was having. In almost every one of them, I wrote, "I finally managed to get away from the grind for a long rest. It's everyone's dream, but I really never expected to make it come true."

I left the hospital reluctantly. When I stepped out of the door, the Dorraines were waiting for me. So was a Shield, an Operator cop from the Washington state council. The Shield informed me that he was there to protect me until I had passed the state line. I attributed his presence to the interference of the Operators at the hospital, and I was tempted to circuit around the state on buses indefinitely.

Once we had left Washington, the Dorraines got busy and recruited Flies for The Game. Headaches, which I attributed to Dorraine, plagued me again. I was less concerned with the pain than I was with the damage he might be doing to my head.

THE LUMBERJACKS WANTED TO PURCHASE ME AND
OFFERED TWO HUNDRED POINTS.

I arrived in Butte, Montana, where Dorraine got into The Game with an Operator who said that his name was Don and that he belonged to an organization called The Lumberjacks. He appeared to be distressed at my predicament and when he learned that the experiment had been authorized by a bill of resuscitation issued by Greyhound, he became excited and left. About an hour later while I was brushing my teeth in a hotel room, a picture of five men and two women, each dressed in a red and black plaid jacket, flashed in front of my eyes.

"Who are they?" asked Mrs. Dorraine.

"A crew of Operators from Don's organization," said her husband. "I can't seem to contact them although they're sending in their pictures clearly enough. Extend and see what you can get."

After a moment a voice said, "We're from The Lumberjacks. We want in."

"I'll pick you up in the lobby, "Dorraine said. "I can't give you my room number or this Thing might plant a bomb in it." He came back with The Lumberjacks in tow. The Lumberjacks wanted to purchase me and offered two hundred points. Dorraine argued over price. In the middle of the discussion I fell asleep and awoke to hear a babble of voices in my ears.

"Listen," said one of the voices. "It's awake. Whether we ask for an adjudication here or in Salt Lake is something we can't decide now, anyway. One thing is for sure, we won't get anywhere unless we coach this Thing so that it knows what to do."

Another voice took it from there. "We think this bill of resuscitation is lousy," he told me. "It's just the kind of thing Greyhound would pull. They've got too damn much power. We've been trying to put a crimp in them for a long time and we never had a better chance than with this bill they issued for you. We're going to take up your case and fight it for you."

No Operator had ever said anything more pleasant since Operators had started talking to me. I expressed my appreciation and asked what I could do to help.

"You can do your bit when the time comes," the Lumberjack

went on. "We took a drain on you and got most of your story. Now listen—"

The Lumberjacks, an organization of over a hundred Operators, intended on presenting a petition to a state council, requesting an adjudication—an Operators' legal trial—where they planned to protest the issuance of the bill which they considered dangerous.

Couldn't they also contend, I asked, that I did not need resuscitation?

"That's risky," the Lumberjack told me. "Bills of resuscitation are issued only when a Thing is almost dead. Whether or not you reached that stage is something we can't prove. If we claim you didn't need resuscitation, Greyhound may claim you did, and the adjudicator might hold up the decision for months while he looked into your past."

It occurred to me that power and prestige were important weapons in the world of Operators and that Greyhound might be an organization difficult to defeat.

"You're saying a mouthful," said the Lumberjack. "And we don't expect to win easily. We're asking for the adjudication for next Sunday but we don't know which state to request it in. Utah seems best. In Salt Lake they're strict about operating and we think they will put an end to that bill in a hurry."

I was delighted.

"Of course," the Lumberjack went on, "the Mormons might put an end to you, too. But that's a chance you'll have to take."

THE GREYHOUND DEPOT WAS CROWDED WHEN
WE ARRIVED IN SALT LAKE. "WE CERTAINLY DREW AN
AUDIENCE," THE LUMBERJACKS' LEADER TOLD ME.

I could see that the Mormon Operators, even though they might disapprove of Hadley's experiment, would probably also disapprove of a Thing with a head full of knowledge concerning Operators. I weighed the situation, decided that I had a dubious chance of remaining in the land of living in any case, and decided to give the Lumberjacks a chance.

The Greyhound depot was crowded when we arrived in Salt Lake. "We certainly drew an audience," the Lumberjacks' leader told me. "The trial is set for noon. Check into a hotel and come back."

I was back in the depot at twelve. The adjudication opened with a speech from the Lumberjacks' lawyer, one which sketched in the background of the case and which developed the following argument: If this experiment were permitted, no other similar experiment could be refused; should a sufficient number of Things be permitted to obtain similar information, the world might soon be filled with Things whose knowledge would endanger the very basis of the world of Operators and Things.

I was uneasy. Undoubtedly, the Lumberjack attorney's attack was sure-fire, but it ruined my chances of survival as surely as if he had written a death warrant for me.

Greyhound's attorney made a poor showing. When the request for a bill of resuscitation had been made, he said, the facts of the experiment had not been made clear. Greyhound had granted its bill believing that a much more innocent experiment had been intended. I dreaded the adjudicator's question, "How much has this Thing already learned about Operators?" the answer to which might well seal my fate. But the question never materialized.

"They're draining you all the time," one of the Lumberjacks hissed into my ear. Sit back and relax. Everything is wonderful."

The Lumberjack's lawyer followed Greyhound's statement with a withering comment on the bus company's inefficient and slipshod method of granting bills, and requested that the company be deprived of its privilege of granting any type of document until an official investigation had been made into their practices. Before he had finished his speech I was wondering if I wouldn't be in more danger from Greyhound, before the adjudication was over, than I would be from the adjudicator.

At three o'clock, the adjudication was recessed until the following morning and I returned to the hotel. The Lumberjacks ordered a case of Scotch to celebrate and became uproariously drunk. An Operator representing the hotel complained about the noise and one of the Lumberjacks immediately stoned him. Stoning, I discovered, was a mental process by which one Operator could put another out of commission temporarily. Several hotel Operators appeared on the scene and stoned two of the Lumberjacks. The stoning party went on for hours. By midnight, most of the Lumberjacks were too weak from stoning to remain tuned in on me and I was left with only the voices of the Lumberjacks' leader and one of his assistants.

In the comparative quiet, I reviewed my situation, decided that it was precarious, phoned Western Airlines, determined when I could get the first plane out the following morning, and went to bed. I awoke the next day to discover that the adjudication had been resumed and concluded that morning, and that the bill of resuscitation had been revoked.

"What's more," the Lumberjacks' leader told me, "we got you off rather neatly. The adjudicator was horrified when he heard about Hadley's freak collection, and he's afraid that the collection may contain other Things like you. We promised him that we'd go with you to California and fight your freak status to the end."

Only the Lumberjacks' leader and an assistant named Bost accompanied me. I flew to San Francisco and took a bus (not Greyhound) to the city which had been identified as the location of Hadley's organization, and checked into a hotel while the Lumberjacks contacted Hadley's organization.

Almost immediately, Nicky's voice joined those of the Lumberjacks. He was startled at the course which events had taken and hustled away to report to Hadley. Bost also hurried off to file a petition for a new adjudication.

NO SOONER HAD I MOVED IN THAN I
DISCOVERED I WAS ONLY A FEW STEPS FROM THE BUILDING IN
WHICH HADLEY'S ORGANIZATION WAS LOCATED...

Nicky returned quickly. "So long as you're going to stay here for a while," he said, "you might as well rent a furnished apartment."

This seemed sensible and I walked down the block he indicated and turned into a building which advertised furnished apartments.

No sooner had I moved in than I discovered I was only a few steps from the building in which Hadley's organization was located, and that the street I was on housed Hadley's freak collection. Only the assurances of the Lumberjacks prevented me from moving out a few minutes after I moved in.

The Operators from Hadley's organization tuned in, and meeting them took most of the afternoon. Finding them surprisingly good-natured, I relaxed considerably, and before the day was over I was talking to them freely. Sharp and Hinton, I learned, were out of town on organization business and the great Hadley was hiding from the California state council which was threatening him with jeopardy because of his freak collection.

The situation, on the whole, was promising. The next day I received additional good news. Hadley, sentenced to jeopardy for a year, had fled and the organization was temporarily under the leadership of The Duck, an easy going Operator with a sense of humor and a generally benign attitude toward Things.

The Operators in Hadley's organization, I learned, were known locally as The Western Boys and were held in considerable fear by other local Operators. Despite their reputation, I found The Western Boys likable. They buzzed in and out, questioned me at great lengths concerning my reactions to the world of Operators and appeared to be amused at my responses.

One of them, an Operator named Winkle, named me This One. "Come in and listen to This One," he'd say, whenever he got me into a discussion. "It's sounding off again." It was Winkle who decided that my attitude was the result of my being a natural bronco. "A horse would worry itself sick," he said. "Broncos never do. Give a bronco something it should worry about and instead it kicks you in the teeth."

"Not entirely," Nicky told him. "This One was a natural bronco and it's gradually getting back to its original personality. But, also, there's been an anchor in This One ever since the experiment started." To me, he explained, "An anchor is something like a permanent sedative. It quiets your nerves. With an anchor in, all of your emotional responses are kept at low key."

Considering that I would have to stay where I was for a time, I was relieved that the emotional environment surrounding me was so favorable. Hadley's Operators were fun and might even be persuaded, I thought, to assist the Lumberjacks in freeing me. That night, when I was getting ready for bed, the only Operator with me suddenly disappeared. A few seconds later, a feminine voice started to whisper into my ear.

"I'm not a member of Hadley's organization. I just live in the building. You can call me Grandma. Everyone does. You mustn't worry. We have some very nice people in this building and they'll try to keep an eye on you. I'll drop in whenever I can and see how you're doing." Her voice faded away. I fell asleep, comparatively serene.

Before the week was over, an Operator named Crame purchased The Western Boys from Hadley. "He's a bastard," one of the Operators told me, "but we'll protect you as much as we can."

Crame tuned in early one morning when I was eating breakfast. He also projected a picture of himself, a somewhat reckless action, I thought, inasmuch as he was living a few doors away. Projecting the picture, I decided, was a scare tactic. He was a mountain of a man with a square, cruel face. I eyed him with the same fishy-eyed detachment with which he eyed me.

"It's a damned inconvenience," he roared, and it was a moment before I realized that the "it" he was referring to was myself. His opening gambit confused me momentarily but I gathered my wits together and reminded him that the same fate which had overcome the great Hadley might also await him.

"It's too damned impertinent," he bellowed. "Dummetize it." His picture and voice abruptly disappeared.

"I enjoyed listening to you telling him off," an Operator named Wimp told me. "I'd like to do it myself. But you'd have done better if you had kept your mouth shut. Dummetizing won't do you any good."

Nicky seemed heartbroken. "I suppose we have to do it, but I don't want to. Heaven knows how you'll turn out when you're dummetized."

I was apprehensive. What was dummetizing?

"It's a process by which most of a Thing's latticework is removed and new latticework is allowed to grow in," Nicky told me. "Latticework is the growth in your mind which stores your habit patterns. It's called latticework because it looks something like the wooden lattices they use to support rose bushes. Once latticework is removed, new latticework will grow in quickly, but it may be a very different kind of growth. The kind of habits you'll develop will depend on the Operators working on you while it's growing in."

Wimp agreed. "With the crew we've got in this outfit, you may turn out to be quite a kid and then again you may turn out as nutty as a fruitcake."

"Let's take out only a very small section of latticework," an Operator named Rink suggested. "Crame may be satisfied."

Wimp had the best suggestion. "Get The Duck."

The Duck was delighted with the story of my interview with Crame. "I like This One as it is," he said. "Leave its latticework alone. I'll talk Crame out of the dummetizing idea."

Nicky was greatly relieved. "Crame might even have decided to make a complete dummy out of you," he told me, "and that would have been a headache for us. To make a complete dummy, you have to remove all the latticework and continue to scrape away new growth as fast as it grows in. A dummy is entirely at the mercy of its Operator and has to be reminded of everything—baths, brushing its teeth, eating. You almost have to breathe for it."

I was horrified. Why would an Operator want to make a dummy out of a Thing?

"Well, Operators use dummies as hat racks," Nicky explained. "Most of the great comic entertainers are dummies. Bob Hope, for instance. When an entertainer like Hope is performing, he's merely giving out what some Operator is stimulating him to do. There's no latticework to interfere with the receiving of the stimuli. In certain situations, a dummy can be quite an asset to a clever Operator. It's something like having a puppet on a string."

I was still uneasy. If some Operator started to dummetize me, would I be aware of what was happening?

"No," Nicky told me. "Scalloping out latticework is painless. Of course, an Operator who inspected your head afterward could see that you had been scalloped. You'd realize that something had happened to you, too. You'd be pretty foggy. But don't worry. The Duck will protect you."

When I awoke the next day, I was conscious of a sharp pain in the back of my neck. Positive that I was being scalloped, I called frantically for Nicky and The Duck. Both tuned in instantly.

"Nobody's doing anything to you," Nicky said. "I think you've got a rheumatic pain of some kind. Maybe you should invest in a heating pad."

"Or a bottle of Scotch," said The Duck.

A minute after their voices drifted away, Grandma was whispering into my ear. "They're idiots," she said. "You want to go to a doctor. There's something definitely wrong with your neck."

I located a doctor early in the afternoon. Wimp came with me and told me that the doctor was an Operator. "What's more," Wimp said, "he's quite an important Operator with a great deal of power. He may do you a lot of good."

I was surprised to find the doctor pleasant and cheerful. He diagnosed my ailment as an infected mastoid. "It's a good thing you caught it in time," he told me. "An infected mastoid can be very troublesome, if neglected."

I came home grateful for Grandma's protective and sympathetic busybodying.

HADLEY WAS HIDING FROM THE CALIFORNIA STATE COUNCIL, WHICH WAS
THREATENING HIM WITH JEOPARDY BECAUSE OF HIS FREAK COLLECTION.

The Western Boys left me alone frequently and some of the Operators in the building made it a practice to drop in on such occasions. From them I learned a great deal about Rita, the goddess of the sun temple, and Hadley's most famous freak. One afternoon, I even sat in on a workout arranged for Rita.

"Rita was always a nice Thing," Browney, one of the housewives in the building was telling me one afternoon, "but, unfortunately, inclined to drink heavily. Rita's husband is an Operator. He turned over Rita's charter to Hadley, hoping that Hadley could straighten Rita out. Hadley said that the reason he flooded Rita's room with pictures of the sun god was to frighten Rita into sobriety. Of course, when you tried to pin Hadley down, he always could think of some well-intentioned motive for creating any freak."

As soon as Rita saw the sun god, I learned, she fell down on her knees. Soon, she had built an altar in her living room and before long there were a dozen women in there with her, paying homage to the sun god. When the congregation got a bit large for the living room, Rita moved the altar to the garage. Rita's husband was furious at Hadley's therapy, but Hadley refused to return the charter.

I was listening intently when a strange voice came in. "Browney, are you with This One?"

"Sally? Come in. There's only Vera and I."

"Listen," said Sally. "Cameron, Jocko and the Spider are going to have a workout on Rita at four o'clock. There's a latch into This One's apartment from Crame's apartment and if we can find it and tune in we might be able to hear."

"I can arrange it," Browney told her. "This One, sit in the living room on the sofa. That's where the latch is. You'll be tuned in on Crame's room and we can tune in on you and hear what's going on."

I wanted to know about the latch. "It's a listening beam," Vera told me. "It can be done mentally, and most Operators keep a latch in on a Thing when the Thing is asleep, but Crame's boys do it with equipment. That's why the boys usually tell you to sit on the sofa. In that way, they can talk to you without having to extend."

At four o'clock, I was sitting on the sofa. Pictures of three unfamiliar faces flashed before my face. One of them was swarthy and malevolent. "That's the Spider," Browney said. There was, I noticed, beneath his dark evil face, a bright bow tie.

"What I want to know," said Vera, "is why the workout?"

"Rita's having doubts again," Sally told her. "It's a darn shame. If they left Rita alone, Rita would snap out of that sun god business right away. But just as soon as Rita gets doubts, they work it up again."

The women could hear and see a great deal more than I could. Browney had to keep me informed on the activity. I continued to see the men's faces, however, and I noticed that they seemed to be standing near a window.

"Rita lives in the house across the street from Crame and they're working on Rita through the window," Browney told me. "By the rules, as soon as a Thing starts having doubts about some delusion which an Operator has successfully injected, it has to be given a fair chance to throw the delusion off. A workout is arranged and the Thing is given an opportunity to be persuaded either way. In this workout, the Spider is going to try to convince Rita that there really is a sun god and Cameron is going to try to convince Rita that the whole business is just a delusion. I don't know what Jocko is doing."

"He's keeping score," Sally said. "Maybe Rita's husband complained to the city council and the council ordered that an official score be sent to them."

"Can you see Rita's husband anywhere?" Vera asked.

"No," Sally said, "but you can bet he's on another latch somewhere. Let's keep quiet. I want to get an idea of their techniques. I understand that the Spider is very clever."

I heard comments from Browney and her friends but I could hear nothing of the workout. Browney said, finally, "Well, that's that. Cameron was trying to convince Rita how absurd it was to think that a sun god would single it out for communication. Rita was feeling quite humble and Cameron almost had it over the line. Then the Spider came in and told Rita that the sun god had to have some mortal to re-establish him and that Rita should feel grateful and humble to be so honored. Rita just carried over the feeling of humility into that channel. Well, it's a change, anyway. Instead of being vain about the honor of tending the temple, Rita feels humble about it."

"Poor Thing," Sally said. "When does Rita's husband get the charter back?"

"Not for six months," Vera said. "He'll probably cure it of that nonsense right away and then it will start drinking again. I don't know why he sticks to that Thing."

"Because of the children," Sally said. "I never approved of Operators marrying Things for that reason. You never know what your children are going to be, for one thing, and even when they're Things, you're fond of them because they're yours. And if you're married to a Thing whom your children like, and he turns out to be a lout, there you are, stuck."

Crame's latch, I noticed, if it ran straight from Crame's building to my sofa, also ran right down the middle of my bed. No wonder they can hear me if I awake in the night, I thought. They must have someone on that listening beam all night to make sure I don't run away.

I had a detached feeling about the goddess of the sun temple. But concerning another of Hadley's experiments, I was furious.

The Costello girl was fifteen and highly introverted. Hadley had won her charter one night in The Game and he had turned her into a monstrosity worthy of his collection. He had used the English language to accomplish the feat, a bitter touch, as the girl apparently spent most of her time reading.

"Hadley convinced the girl that this planet is really purgatory," Browney told me, "and that it was populated with souls working their way to Heaven. All the misfortunes that befell people, he convinced it, were cleansing fires which wiped out immature traits in their make-up. After he had laid this framework, he convinced it that newspapers and books contained code messages from devil to devil and that this was their method of communicating with each other. He rammed a simple code language into its head. I have the code around, somewhere. Words like "small," "little Joe," and "animal" were supposed to refer to souls. Words like "anglers" and "fishermen" were supposed to refer to devils. Words with a hard "I" sound, like "fire" and "eye," referred to the torments inflicted by the devils."

"I'm beginning to think Hadley has a religious complex himself," I said.

"Well," Browney told me, "it's one of the best subjects to use in planting delusions. Anyway, this Costello kid is really nuts by this time. Mrs. Costello is frantic and has been to the city council. Of course, Hadley claims he was trying to straighten out the girl."

"But there are many neurotic adolescents. Most of them get straightened out before they grow up. How could Hadley do a thing like that to a young girl."

Browney agreed sympathetically. "Since Hadley left, Mrs. Costello has been pouring sedation into the kid and letting it rest because it's really on the verge of a mental breakdown."

I discussed the Costello girl with Nicky. "How did you hear about that?" he wanted to know. "That flock of hens in the building, I suppose. I want to warn you of something. There's a Shield on this beat named Brannigan. He's friendly with Mrs. Costello and he's been trying to persuade Crame to return the girl's charter to her. In addition, he's petitioned for an adjudication to enforce the return of the charter. We think that he'll cite you as an example of what Crame may finally do to the Costello girl. You'll have Brannigan snooping around here and you'd better be cautious with him."

One evening Mrs. Costello brought Brannigan to talk to me. Brannigan impressed me as being a hard hitter, a good guy to have in one's corner. I was even more favorably impressed with Mrs. Costello. There was a fineness and sensitivity about her that was rare among Operators, and her grief over her daughter moved me tremendously. I told Brannigan most of my story, omitting all mention of the Lumberjacks. I tried to impress him with the fact that my own life was in jeopardy and that while I was anxious to be free of my experimental status, I wasn't anxious to be killed by the council because of my knowledge of Operators.

Brannigan snorted. "Who told you that! Any Operator can induce amnesia and destroy your memories any time he chooses. Don't let The Western Boys kid you. They're not worried about your life. They're worried about themselves. At that, you don't know as much about Operators as you think you do. You're familiar with some of their techniques but you don't even know a fraction of those. The main thing is that you've never gone around discussing what you do know with other Things and that will impress the council."

That evening the Lumberjack Operator, Bost, came in to tell me that my adjudication had been postponed. The adjudicator had asked for a full bill of particulars concerning me, and the Lumberjacks felt that it would take the council a month to gather the necessary information about me.

"Where will they get this information?"

"From Operators you knew and from the company you worked for," Bost said. "Our attorney advises that you send in your resignation to your company right away. They're going to be on the hook and they're likely to give a good report of you if you're not on their books, a status which will embarrass them, considering the nature of this experiment."

That evening I sent an official resignation to my company. I felt sad about it because I had planned to return. I came home to find Hinton's voice waiting for me.

"Thank God," he said. "You finally got that place out of your future."

I remembered Burt and for a moment I wished that I might be able to see Hinton's head. I would have thrown something at it.

"Sophisticated is coming back," Nicky told me. "He's expected tonight. You'll like him. He used to be a member of our organization but he couldn't get along with Hadley. The Spider admires him tremendously and asked him to return as soon as Hadley left."

I was doubtful about anyone the Spider would admire and I decided to warm up to Sophisticated by slow and careful stages. But I found him to be such an attractive personality that I capitulated immediately. On the night of his arrival, Sophisticated came in to talk to me and most of the boys came with him. In answer to his questions, I told him how I felt about being a guinea pig in a cage and went into details concerning the leanness of my pocketbook and the injustice of my having to finance the experiment myself.

"Another difficulty," I said, "is that I'm not only living in a cage, I'm living in a crooked cage. This experiment is more difficult for me than the Operators realize. It forces me to live in a double world. It's like having a magic mirror through which I'm observing what's happening on the moon while I'm going about the business of living on the earth."

Sophisticated responded by drawing a series of cartoons about a guinea pig in a cage. A picture of a guinea pig standing on its hind legs, arguing with white-jacketed doctors. A picture of a guinea pig huddled in a corner of its cage, counting its pennies and complaining, "—and I have to feed myself." The cartoons were cleverly drawn and the guinea pig was sketched as an appealing animal. Well, I thought, I seem to amuse Sophisticated as much as I do the other Operators and, considering the circumstances, that's as good an impression as I can hope to make.

About my personal situation, Sophisticated was completely detached. "The cage locks you in," he told me, "but it also locks you out. In having to tolerate the Operators, you are free of the necessity of having to tolerate Things. You have gained a great deal without appreciating it. The difficulty is that your temperament does not tend to be philosophic but, instead, is entirely engrossed with immediate problems. You need to develop perspective. What I really don't understand about the choice of someone like you for an experiment of this type is that your temperament is the worst kind I can imagine for the purpose."

"But This One is typical of American Things," Nicky told

him. "That was one of the chief reasons Hadley decided to use it. Another factor is that it normally keeps its business to itself and we didn't have to worry about its blabbing about this experiment to other Things."

"This One may be typical of the American personality in that it tends to use will factors and to take action about such problems as it gets into. But don't tell me that Hadley was primarily interested in knowing how American Things would react to the knowledge that Operators controlled them."

"It was one of his objectives," said Sharp. "He was concerned about the research that's going on about us in that university. He was afraid that they had made so much progress, they might stumble upon the truth. Frankly, the American temperament being what it is, I don't think the truth would even register. American Things just wouldn't accept it."

"Just how did Hadley intend to resolve this experiment," Sophisticated asked.

"It hadn't been worked out in detail," Nicky said. "He planned to give This One a complete indoctrination, have it confined in an institution, and let it work its way out. He assumed that it would tell all it knew and that this would bring about any of a variety of reactions. For one thing, the story, coming from a mental patient and preceding any information which might come from that university, would tend to discredit the university's findings. Of course, the difficulty with his plan was that This One would be unlikely to talk if it were faced with psychiatrists, knowing that its statements would be interpreted as the ravings of a madwoman."

After the boys had gone, I thought about Hadley's plan and wondered to what extent Crame intended to develop it. In the middle of my reflections, the soft voice of Grandma rustled in my ear. "Listen," she said, "it's one thing to tell a story like that inside a sanitarium and quite another thing to tell it to a psychiatrist whose office you're visiting and to whom you're paying money. You must realize by this time that your silence is Crame's greatest asset. If you talked, this experiment might stop right away. Look in a phone book, pick out a doctor, make an appointment, and go to see him."

I located the listing for psychologists and selected a name at random.

"Quick," Grandma said, "write this down somewhere. 'Should I ever lose my memory, it is important for me to remember that I am never, under any circumstances, to return to the company that employed me.'"

"What makes you think I'll lose my memory," I asked her.

"That's one of the few ways they can get you off alive. My guess is that even if the Lumberjacks win the adjudication for you, the adjudicator will enforce a sentence of amnesia on you."

After Grandma had departed, I speculated on her reasons for cautioning me against resuming the job I had been doing. Burt, I thought. None of them ever did like Burt. It was all very discouraging. Despite my rising hopes of escaping from the cage, it was clear that my world as I had known it was being destroyed by circumstances beyond my control and that I should have to fashion a new one for myself when I returned to the world of Things.

Nicky came in one day to tell me that Wimp Semple was being assigned to me permanently. "I've asked him to pay special attention to your personal needs," Nicky said. "You're becoming forgetful. You forgot to brush your teeth this morning and you didn't put up your hair last night. You can't become careless. You'll look like a frump."

I was disturbed because I realized that Nicky's statements were true. I was becoming increasingly forgetful, even of the mechanical routines of grooming. A horrible thought struck me.

Nicky sighed. "Yes," he said, "that's right. You've been partially dummetized. Crame insisted upon it and the Spider did it one night while you were asleep. Quite a few of your habit patterns have disappeared. Don't worry about it. New habit patterns will develop as soon as the new latticework grows in. And Wimp will make sure that all necessary patterns are included."

Dummetized. It was a blow. And suppose the Spider decided to make a complete dummy of me? I wrote the doctor's phone number on a large piece of paper and tacked it to the wall near the telephone. If my forgetfulness increased, I'd pay a visit to the doctor and tell him about it.

Wimp Semple was young, about nineteen, not a very bright boy, but gentle and quiet. The first day on the job, he persuaded me to go out for a walk and steered me in the direction of a movie theater. "Let's go relax," he said.

A short distance from the theater, Wimp asked me to stop. "I'm walking two blocks in back of you," he said. "When you get to the drug store on the corner, go in and have a soda. I've got to see somebody who lives near here."

I went into the drug store and ordered a malted.

"What are you doing," said a strange voice in my head.

"I'm having a malted," I thought.

"Who said that," asked the voice.

"This Thing did," said a second voice. "If you're asking what I'm doing, I'm taking a look at this Thing's woodwork. It's the damnedest woodwork I ever saw. You know who I think this is? Crame's 'This One.'"

"I want a look," said Number One.

"No board, no shack, no cover," said Number Two. "They've got it open on a hinge."

"I understand that they keep it wide open most of the time," said Number One." It talks to you if you ask it questions."

"Listen" said Wimp's voice suddenly, "get the hell off the premises."

"It's Wimp Semple," said Number One. "Let's block him off and have a good look at this Thing."

"Christ," said Wimp and his voice disappeared.

I hesitated between running for home and staying where I was. I decided to stay, thinking that I might pick up a few facts about Crame which I hadn't been able to get from The Western Boys.

Number One groaned suddenly, "Stoned. I'm getting out. I can't stone back. I'm not loaded."

"Well, I am," said Number Two, "I got a load of stuff a few minutes ago and I'll use it on whoever tries to get me." In a few minutes, his screams rang in my ears.

"Well, they're gone," said Wimp. "Golly, so many people in this town have heard about This One, you can't even walk down the street with it, without some damn busybody trying to come in."

"Anybody else around here want his damned head stoned off?" said a new high-pitched voice.

"This is my friend, Frisco," Wimp told me. "He was the guy I wanted to see. He's one of the best stoners in town. He's got such a hard head he can't be stoned even if a mob of Operators gang up on him."

"Those two jerks are from Conroy's organization," Frisco said, "and they might be back with some more of their mob. Where were you taking this Thing?"

"We've got to call it This One," Wimp told him. "The Duck thinks it sounds nicer and he doesn't want to hurt its feelings. He gave me orders to take it to a movie and that's where I'm going. But I'm afraid those hushheads might come back and go for me."

"I'll come to the movie with you," Frisco said. "I'm not doing anything in particular." We proceeded to the theater where I was pleasantly surprised to find that the feature was Walt Disney's *Vanishing Prairie*.

"All about animals and stuff," said Frisco. "You two sit down and enjoy it. I'll keep my eyes open for trouble."

A cartoon was flashing on the screen when I walked into the theater. Before it had finished, Conroy's Operators were back looking for vengeance. The first evidence that they were getting it was Wimp's anguished scream. "They got me," he said. "I gotta get out. Listen, This One—"His voice stopped abruptly.

"Stay where you are, This One," Frisco said. "I'll finish off these characters." A bedlam of voices suddenly rushed in on my ears. Petrified, I sat in my seat and waited. I could hear Frisco's high-pitched voice rising above the bedlam and I decided that I was reasonably safe so long as I continued to hear him. The voices became fewer and fewer until only Frisco's yelling remained. After a while his screams slid down to a lower key.

"I was loaded to the hilt," he said in a satisfied voice. "I sure took care of that bunch. There'll be a lot of headaches in Conroy's organization tonight. You sit where you are and I'll give Wimp a phone call. He's gone back to Crame's."

The *Vanishing Prairie* was over before it occurred to me that I had heard nothing from Frisco in over an hour. Delighted with the silence, I sat through the movie a second time. Considerably relaxed, I came home. At the doorway, Frisco's voice said, "Well, I delivered you safe and sound. I had a good sleep myself. Be seeing you around."

Wimp's voice, hoarse but recognizable, said, "Thanks, Frisco. Come in, This One. Rink is going to take you over for the night. I'm not able to operate."

Rink listened to my account of Frisco's battle with Conroy's mob.

"What did Frisco mean when he said he was loaded to the hilt?" I asked.

"He had probably just bought a load," Rink told me. "It's the stuff Operators stone with. You get it at any drug store. It comes in little tablets and when an Operator swallows a few, he's charged with the kind of energy he needs to stone with."

I remembered the conversation of Conroy's men. "They said my head was open on a hinge."

"It was, then," Rink said. The picture of the outline of a head flashed before my eyes. "I'm projecting a picture so you'll understand this. When a Thing's mind is open on a hinge, the cells around the outside of the mind are closed tightly except for a little section at the top." An invisible knife cut into the head as if it were a pie and removed a thin slice.

"When the mind is opened wide, the rest of the cells are opened." The slice widened until it was the size of three quarters of the head. "When a Thing's mind is wide open, dozens of Operators can get in easily. If an Operator is using a Thing as bait, the mind is always kept wide open. Nothing attracts an Operator like a wide-open head. He can't resist it."

"Conroy's men said there was no board or shack on my mind."

"Of course not," Rink told me. "Boarding and shacking are processes which seal the cells about the mind and so prevent any Operator from getting in. Of course, Operators don't resort to either boarding or shacking unless the Thing's mind can't be shut. A mind that is shut has been closed and then locked with a special mental code that no one knows except the Operator who is operating the Thing. Most Things are protected from other Operators by a shut head."

"Has my head been damaged so it can't be shut?"

"Frankly, I think it has been. However, it's nothing to worry about. Heads can always be mended by one process or another."

"Rink, would you show me a picture of latticework?"

Obligingly, he drew an inner circle inside the outline of the head, about an inch from the rim. "All of that is latticework. Sometimes, the latticework is allowed to grow in much thicker—it depends upon the number of patterns the Thing needs. What they've done in your head has been to scrape some of the latticework away on the sides. Of course, most Things depend on their habit patterns to get them through their daily activities when an Operator isn't around to stimulate them. You'd be surprised at how little thinking is done by Things. Most of them just follow patterns some Operator has carefully cultivated in their heads. When latticework is scraped away, a Thing finds that he can't think too well. But actually it's not his thinking ability that has been affected. It's just that he has depended upon habit patterns instead of upon thinking."

"How much latticework do they take off when they make a full dummy?"

Another head outline came into view. The inner line this time extended only across the top of the skull and only for a distance of about half an inch.

"That's a dummy with a top knot," said Rink. "And whenever an Operator runs into one of those, he knows that the Thing is not responsible for anything it does. It's being controlled entirely by an Operator. A Thing's control is in its habit patterns. When it has nothing but its thinking ability left, the most feeble Operator can control it, because Things can think only to a very limited degree."

"How limited?"

"I'll tell you this," Rink said with finality. "If it weren't for Operators, Things would still be wandering in and out of caves."

The Lumberjacks appeared suddenly to remind me that my adjudication would be held within ten days. "Another thing," Bost told me. "We've been able to buy a part of your operating time. We hired a local Operator, a woman named Hazel. She'll come in to operate you for us."

Hazel came in before he left. She was a rough and ready individual with a voice like a booming bell. I liked her immensely. She was obviously an individual who wasn't going to be easily frightened by Crame and just as obviously a person who preferred action to talk. I enjoyed her and was delighted when she came back every afternoon. Wimp detested her and would usually clear out as soon as she appeared, and come back in a sulk after she had gone.

Hazel never missed an opportunity to criticize Crame's boys and she told me many stories to illustrate their shortcomings. After one of these discussions Wimp came in, bristling with anger.

"I was listening to what she was telling you," Wimp said. "She makes Crame's outfit sound like a bunch of dogs. What she doesn't explain is that what they do is just plain hook operating. There's nothing wrong with it."

I wanted to know more.

"Well, all operators play the hook game," Wimp explained. "There isn't a better way of keeping your wits sharp. Two Operators try to get each other in a position where one of them is in a spot and has to pay his opponent to get him off. For instance, that Operator across the street, Herb Clarkson. The other day a Thing was killed in an ordinary accident. He fell downstairs and broke his neck. Herb bet a friend of his, Fred, that he could make it look as if Fred had killed the Thing. Fred took him on. Herb maneuvered Fred into making a few comments that really made it appear as if Fred had had something to do with the Thing's death and the Shield who covers this beat, Brannigan, went after Fred.

Fred had to pay Herb twenty points to get Herb to explain. If he'd had more time, Fred would have tried to incriminate someone else and get himself off the hook. That kind of maneuver is allowed in all hook operating. Now, if Herb hadn't been able to get Fred on the hook, he would have had to pay Fred twenty points. That's the way hook operating works. When Hazel tells you about some of the stuff the boys pull, she doesn't explain that it's all perfectly legal. There's nothing wrong with it. It's just plain hook operating."

It sounded pretty grim to me. Did all Operators play at hook operating?

"Sure, if they have enough wits. Besides, it's profitable. With Crame, it's big business. He has one of the best group of Hook Operators in the state. And he's got a system."

What kind of system?

"Well, Crame keeps files on almost every Operator in town. Let's say that Crame hears about an Operator we'll call *F* who has just made a few thousand points. Crame plans strategy to get those points. Now, if the boys went after *F*, *F* would realize they were after his points and he'd avoid playing. The trick is to get *F* on the hook without *F* suspecting that Crame's outfit has anything to do with it.

"So, Crame's boys find out who *F*'s friends are. They start with an Operator we'll call *A* and get *A* on the hook. Then they wait. *A* finds another Operator whom he can pass the hook to. He finally passes it off to *B*. *B* goes after *C*. *C* goes after *D*. Crame's boys watch the action carefully until it reaches *F*. Then they close in on *F* and use strategy to increase the size of the hook. By the time they've finished, the hook is as big as a house and the only person who can get *F* off the hook is Crame and Crame makes the price high."

Operators just preyed on each other.

"It looks that way to you because you're just a Thing and that's the way you've been taught. But it's all perfectly legal with Operators. That Hazel! She's the one who's doing something un-ethical trying to make you think that hook operating is illegal."

HAZEL JOINED US BEFORE I BOARDED THE BUS.
"CHRIST," SHE SAID, "PASADENA! WHAT A PLACE
TO GO. I'M COMING ALONG. WIMP, WHO TOLD
YOU TO USE THE COMPULSE?"

In the slight silence that followed, Sophisticated's raspy chuckle rang like a doorbell.

"Our Wimp is quite a talker. I should never have suspected it. I bear tidings, Wimp. The mighty Crame is on the hook."

"You're kidding," Wimp said.

"Wish that I were, or that I had Crame on the hook myself. Unfortunately I, too, am in danger of being on the hook at any moment. I am packing my bags for a visit to other parts."

"You're running!" Wimp sounded baffled and scared. "What's happened?"

"I suggest that you drop This One and report to headquarters. Crame has already flown and Cameron has gone with him. It seems that two of the—er—mortals they were working on committed suicide last night and somebody seems to think that Crame's organization is responsible. The council is outraged." His voice dropped to a whisper. "One of the—er—mortals was an important technician and quite valuable. You know what the penalty is for that. Auf wiedersehen, my dear Wimp, and you, too, my dear This One. May your futures be bright and your hearts happy."

Wimp disappeared.

Browney tuned in. "What was that all about?" she wanted to know.

I was mute. If Operators retaliated upon Operators by attacking each other's Things, as I had heard was often the case, I might expect an attack from one of the Operators whose Thing had committed suicide. I wondered what to do and while I wondered, set about packing my bags.

Hazel caught up with me before I had finished packing. "Take it easy," she told me. "We've got a few things to do and I can't go running after you if you blow town."

I explained what I was concerned about. "Hell, you're no good to anybody dead," she told me. "Unpack those bags and sit down and have a cup of coffee."

"But suppose the Operator of one of those men who

committed suicide comes after me."

"I'll take care of him, if he does. Let me tell you, there will be jeopardies right and left in Crame's outfit for the next few days and we might be able to profit by it. Never run out on a situation when there's action starting."

Wimp came back. "They're as nervous as cats," he told us. "I'm sticking close to This One. This One is my alibi. It's been a full-time detail for me and I didn't have anything to do with that other stuff. Believe me, for once I'm glad I've been working on one of the freaks."

I knew about compulse but I failed to recognize it when an Operator used it on me. "When you can't get a Thing to do something," Nicky once had told me, "you use compulse and force it."

I awoke in the middle of the night with fear at my throat. "Pack," said Wimp. "Pack fast. You have almost no time." The fear rising in me was not a reaction to his statement but seemed to be welling up like a geyser from some independent source. I packed in a fever, phoned a cab, and went to the bus depot.

Hazel joined us before I boarded the bus. "Christ," she said, "Pasadena! What a place to go. I'm coming along. Wimp, who told you to use the compulse?"

"I was told, that's all," Wimp said, sulkily. "You got your car with you? If you haven't you can ride with me."

"I'd just as soon," said Hazel. "So, things are getting hot, are they? Suppose This One turns around when it gets to Pasadena and comes right back?"

"I keep using compulse every time it tries to come back. I got my orders. Western has every damned Thing it owns on the move."

I looked forward to a ride of relative peace, but no sooner had I boarded the bus than my head began to ache.

"It's an Operator named Kash," Hazel said. "He used to work for Hadley once and Hadley threw him out. He attacks any Thing he can get at that belongs to Western. He's on the bus. If we can get the car close enough, I'll stone his head off."

Kash stoned Wimp.

"Listen, you damned hyena," Hazel yelled at him. "I'll get you jeopardy if you don't keep off this Thing."

I remembered Greyhound's policy of protection for Operators. "Why don't you complain to the driver?" I asked Hazel.

"Because there's some damn Thing driving the bus. That happens once in a thousand trips and it has to be this trip."

The headache increased and my head burned and throbbed. Hazel's voice disappeared abruptly. I never did hear Kash. Apparently he reserved his energies for his activities on my head. At the Pasadena station, Hazel's voice caught up with me, along with Wimp's hoarse whisper.

"Every synapse in This One's head has been broken," Hazel said. "I've got a Shield on Kash's tail and he'll get something for this, believe me."

My head was a live anthill. "What happens when synapses get broken?"

"They get repaired," Hazel said brusquely. "And Crame foots the bill for it. Kash is a lout. He could have killed you."

Wimp, apparently, was also investigating my head. "Jeez," he said, "Jeez, don't look."

After a minute, Hazel said slowly, "Well, it'll take time, that's all. It'll take time."

"Time for what?" Fear was at me again. Not compulse, this time, but my own fear.

"He scalloped you right down to the bone," Wimp said. "You've got a top knot left."

Dummy. I had somehow known it was coming.

I came back on the next bus, calm, almost dead. The worst had happened and there was nothing to be concerned about now.

Browney and the other housewives came to peek into my head and to condemn Kash. "Don't worry about it," Browney told me. "It'll take months for the latticework to grow back but you'll be all right in time."

I tried to remember the date of the coming adjudication and couldn't. I tried to think of the names of Crame's Operators and couldn't. I wondered if I had developed amnesia and located the papers I had prepared for the occasion, and read them over and over.

"It's not amnesia," Wimp told me. "It's because you're a dummy. Read a book or something."

I couldn't read. Words made no sense. I went to a movie but couldn't follow the action of the picture. I had difficulty sleeping. I visited the doctor finally and he prescribed a strong sedative.

When I awoke one morning, only Hinton was around. "They're gone," he said laconically. "Crame's outfit is a shambles."

This was good news but I seemed to have nothing with which to respond emotionally. Besides, there was little to choose between Crame's outfit and Hinton.

Hazel came in. "Quick," she said, "write this address down. Go there if things get rough. You can get an emergency adjudication there, if it's necessary." I wrote the address on a scrap of paper and put it in my change purse.

"What are you planning to do?" Hazel asked Hinton.

"I'm not sitting around for the city council to make a decision on the bill of particulars," Hinton said. "I'm going to rush the action."

"Rush it how?"

"I know a guy." He was quiet for a moment. "Get the telephone directory," he told me. I turned, as he directed, to the listing of churches in the classified section. He indicated a name. "Go there and see the minister. First, write out a list of Operators' terminology with definitions. I'll dictate it. When you see him, show him the material and tell him that Operators' voices have explained the terms to you." *

I typed out the list of terms, he dictated, my mind dull and my spirits low. Dummy, I kept thinking. Even if Hinton does do something for me, it will be months and months before the latticework grows back and I can navigate.

---

* The text of this document is contained in the Appendix, starting on page 199.

I reached the church and went in and asked for the minister. He was a pleasant, smiling man when I entered his office. He read the papers I gave him and listened to what I had to say. His smile disappeared so rapidly and was replaced by an expression of such horrified concern that I found myself feeling sorrier for him than I did for myself.

It took him a while to get his breath. He said, finally, "Why did you come to me?"

I told him that Hinton had sent me. We discussed that for a while. After a time he seemed to get his wits together. "I'm going to call a friend of mine who knows a psychiatrist in the county hospital," he told me. "I'll ask him to make an appointment for you." He made some phone calls and talked to me for a while, urging me to keep the appointment at the hospital on the next day.

"Be sure to bring those definitions with you," Hinton said as I started off the next morning. "This will force the final adjudication."

I arrived at the hospital on time, the definitions in my hand. I went in fearfully, thinking, "If this is the final adjudication, I may not come out of here alive."

The psychiatrist read my definitions carefully.

"Do you see the building out there," Hinton said to me. I looked out at what appeared to be a wing of the building I was in.

"They may put you there. Don't have any fears about it. You'll be out in two weeks with your head shut. And while you're in there, no Operator will be able to get at you. It's a refuge."

I looked out at the building hopefully.

"How long have you been living in California?" asked the psychiatrist. I told him.

"In what state did you live before?" I told him.

"Do you hear these voices often?"

"All the time."

"Do you have any close relatives?"

"Some," I said. "But they're in my home state." Besides, I thought, what good can they do? They're Things.

"You haven't been a resident of the county long enough to be entered in our hospital," the psychiatrist said.

"Tell him you have money," Hinton whispered.

"I can pay for hospitalization," I told the psychiatrist.

"At a hundred and twenty-five dollars a week, you may not be able to pay for long. You're going to need care for a long time."

"Tell him your head will be shut within two weeks," said Hinton.

I told the psychiatrist.

He sighed. "There is a free state institution but they won't accept you either, inasmuch as you haven't lived in the state for a year. The best they can do is permit you to stay there until your relatives come for you."

He brooded over the papers I had given him.

"What I suggest," he said finally, "is that you go to your own home town. You have good control. I'll give you the name of a doctor there. Go straight to him and tell him what you told me." He asked his secretary for a directory, looked up a name, wrote it down on a piece of paper, and presented me with it. I took it, gave him the ten dollars he asked for and a few minutes later I was out on the street. I could have cried. Safety had been so near.

"Go across the street to the drug store," Hinton said in a tight voice. I looked up psychologists in the classified directory as he suggested, selected one, phoned, and made an appointment. That afternoon, armed with my glossary of Operators' terms, I went to his office. "He's better than nothing," Hinton told me. "He can provide an adjudication, although God knows what kind it will be."

Hinton left me at the door of the building and I went upstairs to the doctor's office. He was, I discovered, not a psychiatrist but a psychoanalyst. The difference meant nothing to me. I gave him the glossary. He read it carefully, listened to my story, gave me a list of phone numbers where I could reach him at all times of the day, and asked me to come back on the following afternoon.

The hour in his office was like balm. Hinton never came near me and the relief of not having to listen to his voice was wonderful. Hinton was waiting for me at the foot of the staircase. As I opened my purse to get cab fare, I came upon the address Hazel had given me. I decided that there was nothing to lose by visiting the address and asked the cabby to take me there. I had never heard of the street but the cab driver seemed familiar with it. He drove to a strange section of town and I found myself, finally, in front of the address wondering how I might find a pretext to enter. I noticed a small sign that said "Chiropractor."

"Go in and tell him about your headaches," Hinton said. "You've got to have something to talk about." I told the chiropractor about my headaches. He almost broke my back and then told me that I was very tense. "You're as tight as a roll of rubber bands," he said cheerfully and broke my back again. I came home and went to bed, suddenly very tired.

I returned to the office of the psychoanalyst every afternoon. On the third visit, the Operators disappeared.

*Part Three*

# The Dry Beach and the Waves

For ten days, the dry beach. My scalp felt strained as if some nerve would break at any moment, but the interior of my head felt empty and dry as if its cells had been hollowed out by a ruthless knife and replaced with a sandy shore. The Spider had scalloped it out, I recalled. Then I remembered that the Operators had been delusions. The terrible world of Operators with their tremendous power over Things did not exist. All of that business had been nothing more nor less than insanity. Insanity. The word hung over the beach and the beach stared at it with a kind of mild surprise. Insanity. It was something like digging at the base of a tree in the backyard and finding no roots at all but, instead, a bed of uranium, a strange substance I had heard about somewhere. It wasn't frightening to find uranium in my own backyard, just mildly surprising. The dry beach stared placidly at the uranium, felt a mild relief that it was uranium and not Operators, stared some more, and yawned.

Alertness, which had never failed me in insanity, seemed now to have completely deserted me. After a few unfortunate experiences in traffic, I avoided streets. I tried sitting in my apartment and reading; the words looked perfectly familiar, like old friends whose faces I remembered perfectly well but whose names I couldn't recall; I read one paragraph ten times, could make no sense of it whatever, and shut the book. I tried listening to the radio but the sounds went through my head like a buzz saw. I walked carefully through traffic to a movie theater and sat through a movie which seemed to consist of a lot of people wandering around slowly and talking a great deal about something or other. I decided, finally, to spend my days sitting in the park watching the birds on the lake.

The dry beach irritated the analyst. He asked me to lie on a couch and to say whatever came into my mind. Nothing came into my mind. Pressed urgently to say something, anything at all, I finally described the ceiling. The analyst waved me off the couch and into a chair facing him, and shot questions at me. The questions made sense but I could think of no answers. "Don't tell me there's nothing going on in your mind," the analyst stormed at me. But there was nothing at all going on in my mind. The analyst fretted and fumed as if he knew perfectly well that there was plenty going on under the sandy shore and he was going to bully until it came out. The dry beach listened to him and hoped in a vague, mild sort of way that if there were anything in the department below, it would please stay there because the quiet was so pleasant.

My face undoubtedly was as blank as my mind. After a while the analyst gave up looking at it and sat back in his chair and gazed out the window and talked. I listened intently, forgot what he said immediately. He warned me frequently against thinking about the Operators, and it was easy to follow this advice. Thoughts about the Operators or about anything else rarely disturbed the quiet of the dry beach. Memories of the Operators occasionally drifted onto the sands but the sands would hold no thought whatever for more than a second. There was no rock, not even a pebble, to which a thought could cling.

I told the analyst that I rarely remembered anything he said, once I had left his office. This was unimportant, the analyst said. My unconscious mind would retain what he said and apply it. I was sleeping fifteen hours out of each day. "You don't need that much sleep," the analyst told me repeatedly. "It's only an escape."

If my unconscious mind heard the advice, it ignored it. I went on sleeping fifteen hours a day as if the department beneath the dry beach which wouldn't come out to argue with the analyst ("It's your unconscious mind," the analyst said irritably, "stop referring to it as anything else") nevertheless knew perfectly well what it was doing and needed advice from no one.

The department beneath the dry beach, besides having cut the connections which attached the beach to thought-producing units, had also severed the last connection with the emotional machinery. "There's an anchor in This One," Nicky had said. The anchor was still in, more securely attached than ever. I walked serenely about the park, undisturbed that I had been insane for six months, undisturbed that I could not now think, undisturbed that I was thousands of miles from home. I stared at the serene swan that swam on the park's lake appreciatively, understandingly.

On the eleventh day, while I was blinking at a traffic signal light, remembering in it something familiar, something which had a meaning I couldn't recall, a wave cascaded on the beach. A physical sensation, it arose in the back of my head and drifted forward in a pleasant way, like a light gentle wash of sea froth. The wave fell, disappeared into the sands and left on the beach a thought. I remembered suddenly the purpose of traffic signals and what the red and green lights meant. I passed a newsstand and saw a newspaper headline which announced that a star had fallen from a window. The dry beach contemplated the headline with mild surprise. How could a big thing like a star get into a window? A wave cascaded gently on the shore and I realized suddenly that the star was probably a Hollywood star. Death of a Salesman, said a movie marquee. The dry beach blinked at the marquee and speculated vaguely that a salesman might be a native of some country named Sales, probably in Asia. Then a wave broke and I remembered that I had read the play and I was aware sharply of the name of the country in which the salesman was a native.

I was grateful for the waves. The waves could remember, deduce, apply insight. The dry beach could not.

# The Subterranean Craftsman

The waves guided me along streets, frequently appeared in the park to clarify small mysteries, but stubbornly stayed underground while I was in the analyst's office. The analyst sputtered in irritation, attempting to get answers to his endless questions. The dry beach stared at him fixedly and tried hard to think of something to say; but the waves stubbornly ignored him. And then, unexpectedly, one day after the analyst had asked me something, a wave cascaded abruptly on the beach. Surprised, I absorbed it and passed it to the analyst. In my youth, I said, I had entertained ideas about writing fiction and had put the ideas away with other toys. Startled at hearing me say anything, the analyst surveyed me for a second, suggested immediately that I write something.

"Write what?"

"Write a novel," he said. "Write anything."

I bought some paper, set up the portable typewriter which I had dragged all over the country with me, and sat down to write. I expected that little would happen. Thinking, any kind of thinking, was almost impossible and I was certain that I would require an entire day to write even a paragraph. To my amazement, while I was staring blankly at the typewriter, a wave broke over the beach leaving on the shore an idea. Startled, I started to write and found that I was composing as fast as I was typing and that I was typing at my normal rate of about sixty words a minute. I typed for two hours and sat back to read what I had written. The material was a little difficult for the dry beach to follow but the story seemed to be about some woman and some man and some people the woman knew who were getting ready to do something or other to the man.

THE WORDS CAME FROM NOWHERE,
SHOT DOWN INTO MY FINGERS, AND APPEARED
MAGICALLY ON THE PAPER.

I brought it to the analyst, who was delighted with it. "Quite an orderly piece of work," he told me, "and clever, in a way. How do you intend to resolve the situation these characters are in?" Inasmuch as I had only the vaguest concept of the situation the characters were in, this was tantamount to asking me how I intended to resolve development on the intercontinental missile. I said, "I don't know yet," which seemed like the safest thing to say and the analyst smiled over the papers again and slipped them into a desk drawer. A wave cascaded over the beach abruptly, indignantly. I demanded the return of the first chapter of my novel. The analyst gave it back to me.

Heartened, I set aside two hours of each afternoon for my new project. It was a weird experience. I was not assisted by the waves and, indeed, there would have been no time for their somewhat slow process. The words came from nowhere, shot down into my fingers, and appeared magically on the paper. I made no mental preparation for the writing periods; the dry beach was incapable of making any preparations, even that of remembering to start writing at two o'clock of each day. At the appointed hour a wave would roll in to remind me that writing time had arrived, I would look at the clock to verify the fact that it was two o'clock— for the beach had only the vaguest idea at any time as to whether it was morning, afternoon, or evening—and I would find, always, that it was exactly two o'clock. Not one minute before two or one minute after two, but exactly two o'clock. Somewhere under the sandy shore, a clock had been built and synchronized perfectly with the clock in my room.

I would sit at the typewriter, put my hands on the keys, and start in. I had almost no comprehension of what I was writing and no memory whatever of what I had written, once I had closed the typewriter. My fingers seemed to know which keys to hit and that was all there was to it. Apparently they were being guided by the department below the sandy shore which contained the knowing waves and the perfectly synchronized clock and which seemed completely capable of forming the waves, operating the clock and writing a novel without any assistance from the dry beach.

On the day when I was scheduled to begin writing the eleventh chapter I took time out to read the ten chapters I had already written. The dry beach apparently had grown a little stronger, for I seemed better able to follow the action of the plot, and I found myself interested in the story as a reader might be and I wondered how the story would end. I speculated about this mildly, and after I had completed writing another chapter, sat down to study what I had written. I discovered, to my surprise, that I seemed to have composed, not the eleventh chapter, but the last chapter. Some of the characters were grey-haired and old and one of them, who had just been born in the tenth chapter, had reached a very active maturity in this chapter.

I related the incident to the analyst hesitantly, as one might discuss witchcraft. He was not particularly impressed. "Undoubtedly," he told me, "your unconscious has already planned the book to its very end and knows, already, everything that will be in it. Professional writers sometimes experience similar phenomena."

I wrote the novel, some sixty thousand words, in about thirty hours. An amateurish effort, it was still better than anything I might have written at any other time. Also, under normal conditions my rate of planning and writing the same thing would have been closer to sixty thousand words in five hundred hours. When I had finished the book, the last chapter fell neatly in place, an inevitable end for the story as it had developed.

# Something

After a month the waves were supplemented by a more disconcerting phenomena, Something. Something told me, after I had reached the street and started to the food market, to return to my apartment. I did, wondering, and found that I had left my purse on the kitchen table. Something urged me to return to the rear of the food market, after I reached the checker's counter, and kept me rooted to one spot looking at one shelf until I finally noticed the item which I had been trying for days to remember to buy. Something urged me to turn up a side street which was out of my way; I did and in the middle of the block found a typewriter repair shop whose services I required. Something urged me violently to turn around and retrace a block I had just walked. I did and found a dollar bill on the sidewalk.

I had been making regular visits to a chiropractor whose treatments I credited with the disappearance of the pain in my scalp. Something urged me to discontinue visits. I mused over this strong urge, realized that the cost of the visits was straining my budget, feared the reappearance of the scalp pains, and decided to continue the treatments. On my way to the next appointment, I got off the bus at the right corner and then discovered that I could not recall the chiropractor's address. I wandered around the neighborhood looking for the building but could not recall what the building looked like. I thought of looking in the telephone directory for the address but as I approached the telephone booth, the chiropractor's name was suddenly blotted from my mind. I went home, upset, nervous, and wondering if the Operators would be walking back into my life at any moment. Upon entering my apartment, I remembered the chiropractor's name and address clearly, recalled the appearance of the building in which his office was located and realized that I had passed it several times while wandering around. I turned on my heels, started off for his office again and by the time I reached the street his name, address, and even the number of the bus I had to take was blotted from my mind. I finally got the idea, came back, recalled the chiropractor's name immediately, and telephoned him and canceled future appointments. Something obviously was determined to have its own way.

I had written down on a scrap of paper the address of a shop which had advertised a sale on shoes. I misplaced the piece of paper and searched for it without success. Something urged me to open the closet door. Wondering, I did. Something urged me to put on my raincoat. I wasn't going anywhere and it wasn't raining. I closed the closet door and continued searching. Something urged and urged. Exasperated, I put on the raincoat, feeling silly. Annoyed, I stuck both hands into the pockets in an angry posture. In one of the pockets was the piece of paper.

Something urged me to write to an old friend whom I had not thought about in years. I ignored the urge. Something nagged and nagged until I sat down and wrote a short note, addressing it to her office. Within a few days I received a letter from her. "I had just opened your letter when [a mutual friend] came in as he does every week to see [her employer] and asked if by chance I knew anything about you as he was trying to get your address to write you concerning [a matter financially beneficial to me]. I was startled as I had just received your letter. I gave him your address. Your letter had so little in it that your address was about the only thing I could tell him about you. . . ."

As my money was running low, I decided that I would try to find a job whose chores were not too demanding. As I started out, Something urged me to walk in the opposite direction from the bus line, toward a large building a few blocks away. Something urged me so violently to enter the building that it would have been impossible, almost, not to have gone in. I went to the building's personnel department and found the employment manager not at all surprised to see me. She had phoned an agency that morning for a receptionist. She hired me.

# Something Extends

Something developed a new trick overnight with the air of one screwing a new attachment onto the machine. I got off the elevator in my apartment house, turned to enter the lobby, and Something, in a lightning burst of illumination, let me know that danger lay around the corner. I walked cautiously, looked about carefully. I turned the corner, caught the eye of the desk clerk, and another stab of illumination struck. I knew instantly what the desk clerk was going to say and even the words she would use in saying it; and I knew, too, what I should say to her to cope with the problem which she was going to present to me. I advanced into the lobby, listened to the desk clerk speak her piece and gave her the answer with which Something had supplied me.

The next day while I was walking from my kitchen to my dressing room, Something burst into another flash of illumination and I was suddenly aware that the maid was about to knock on the door and request permission to enter. I stood rooted before the living room door, wondering, and within a minute or two footsteps came down the hall, a knock sounded on my door and the maid asked if she might come in.

I went through a four-day period of growing apprehension, knowing before people spoke what they would say, knowing, before they turned corners and appeared, that they were coming. A disturbing experience, it left questions on the dry' beach, shook my anchor of calm. When Something started urging me to visit Las Vegas, I was reluctant to go. I made the trip the next weekend, apprehensive, but even more desirous of getting rid of Something's urging. I took five dollars with me and walked about Las Vegas, clutching my money and fearful of gambling it away. Something kept me rooted at one wheel and Something urged me violently to play a certain number at a certain time. I played a dollar chip and won. I waited, rooted, got another strong urge, played, won again. I played six times, won six times, and found myself with a purse full of money. Something stopped giving me numbers. I stopped playing and came home.

Something seemed to have extraordinary talents. I was grateful for the money which was sorely needed, but the anchor was rocking badly. Something abruptly unscrewed its odd attachment and stopped extending.

# My Unconscious Friend

The waves were a gentle and soothing phenomenon, the novel writing was an intriguing experience, but Something frightened me. Something had about it the air of witchcraft. This heavy hand that pushed me steadily to clearly pointed directions— what was it?

Nothing at all to be concerned about, the analyst assured me. Something, like the waves, was coming from my unconscious mind. My mind in schizophrenia had been—well—hurt ("shattered," the dry beach remembered, was the term he had once used) and it was mending. While it was mending, my unconscious was employing methods of aiding me which seemed unusual to me but which weren't, really. They were merely expediences adopted temporarily. In time, Something and the waves would disappear and I would be myself again. What was important was that my unconscious, even if it went about its business in seemingly strange ways, was aiding me, a healthy manifestation.

Even in insanity, the analyst reminded me, my unconscious

had aided me to an extraordinary degree. The analyst, a man not at all impressed by unusual manifestations from the unconscious, seemed to be completely awed by the degree to which my unconscious had aided me throughout schizophrenia. Did I have any idea how many people ever recovered from schizophrenia, even with treatment and long hospitalization? Fewer than half. Did I have any idea how many people recovered from schizophrenia spontaneously, without help? Very, very few. Did I have any idea how unusual it was for someone to go a full six months, wandering around the country as I had done, without care, treatment, or proper rest, to snap out of advanced schizophrenia abruptly as I had done? I was a most unusual case, a freak. The dry beach recalled that the Operators had used the same term for me, a term always resented. I veered away from this discussion of how freakish I was to have snapped out of insanity, which didn't seem particularly freakish to me, and got back to the subject of Something, which was a little too freakish for my taste.

But Something wasn't freakish at all, the analyst insisted. Something was nothing more or less than a provider of hunches, a common enough occurrence among many people, one I probably had been long familiar with in a subtler form. The unconscious, which now was so obviously doing my thinking for me, always had done my thinking for me, but had not been so obvious about it. Something now considered such problems as faced me, thought them out, determined what action to take and, instead of sending a thought into my mind to consider, sent instead a strong urge to take a specific action. If I were completely normal, I would probably refer to Something as a hunch. The urge to write to a friend I had not thought of in years undoubtedly was the result of a course of action already arrived at unconsciously. The friend, even though I had consciously forgotten the fact, came in contact frequently with another friend who traveled constantly and who owed me money, something the unconscious had remembered. The letter had brought about the anticipated result; the friend had forwarded the money. My unconscious, too, had remembered that the slip of paper for which I was searching was in my raincoat and had urged me to get the raincoat from the closet. My unconscious had probably determined that the building toward which it had pushed me was a likely one in which to find a job. The phenomenon of knowing what people were going to say before they spoke? Well, no one knew much about telepathy except that the force apparently existed; at some times, some minds seemed quite capable of reading the minds of others. The six successive wins at Las Vegas? More difficult to explain, the analyst conceded, but still he had heard of stranger phenomena. The weirdness of having my head flooded with winning numbers just before the numbers won was not so unusual as I thought. The unconscious was an awesome instrument and men knew very little about its abilities.

The dry beach considered him in amazement. Was he saying that the unconscious mind could think? The unconscious? Think? The analyst surveyed me with an amused eye. What had manufactured the voices, the personalities of the Operators, woven together the fabric of the world of Operators and Things? What had helped me talk my way out of a mental institution, helped me get away from a mountain lion, talked me into moving off the mountain the next morning?

It was all perfectly clear to the analyst. When schizophrenia had struck, my unconscious had taken over. It had guided me while my mind had been shattered, had even probably aided in the mental repair. It had sensed an approaching recovery and had steered me quickly to a doctor's office where, when my voices left me, I would discover that insanity, not Operators, had overwhelmed me, and where I could cling, with my clouded mind, to a new anchor until the repair work was finished. What I must remember was that my unconscious was a friend, a real friend.

What caused schizophrenia? Well, the great difficulty was that no one knew. It was the greatest medical and psychological problem of the present time. It was a tremendous mystery. Still, still—the analyst contemplated me with a puzzled, irritated eye. The Operators had never seemed to show any concern with sex, had they?

No, the Operators had been businessmen. They had been in the business of operating, as dedicated in their way as a monastery of monks or an office of brokers.

The analyst sighed. Still, still— He glanced at the clock and scheduled me for another appointment. On my next visit, he would continue to explore the cause of my schizophrenia. True, no one knew what caused schizophrenia, but still, still—-

# The Freudian

I returned to the analyst's office for my next appointment with more enthusiasm than I usually felt at such times. This was the day when the analyst would attempt to determine what had brought about my schizophrenia. And even though no one knew what did cause schizophrenia, the analyst appeared to have a knowing glint in his eye, the air of a man who knew a secret or two.

The waves, usually so quiet in the analyst's office, started cascading on the beach as soon as I entered his office. I reminded him immediately that he had promised to explore the cause of my mental collapse and the analyst nodded and plunged right in.

It was simple. Psychoses, in the analyst's opinion, were the result of an inadequate sex life, particularly in America. The analyst was a Frenchman. I asked him what caused schizophrenia in France and the analyst gave me the dirty look he usually gave me when a wave prompted me to ask a question. The only thing he could not understand, the analyst told me, was why, with a full six months at its disposal, my unconscious had not gotten itself into a few thousand discussions about sex.

If Something knew the answer, it kept the answer to itself. No wave helped me. The dry beach considered the question and after a moment was as surprised as the analyst was. True, there had been also a great many other subjects with which my unconscious had not shown any particular concern. It hadn't discussed my friends or my family, or money or marriage, or politics or parents, or death or taxes. It had been concerned only with explaining the workings of the world of Operators.

"It probably has a one-track mind," I said. The analyst blinked at me and I explained. My unconscious was probably an unconscious with a one-track mind. The comment irritated the analyst. That, it appeared, was exactly the point. All unconscious minds were one-tracked. They were singularly one-tracked. They were one-tracked about sex. There was no reason in the world why my unconscious mind should have spent six months talking about Operators and Things when it could have, just as easily, spent six months talking about sex.

The analyst, besides being a Frenchman, was a Freudian. Freudians, I decided later, had much in common with small religious cults, possessed with tight little worlds of ideas, which built little matchstick kingdoms on a wide plateau of truth before claiming the plateau. To the analyst, any breakdown in mental or emotional machinery could be traced only to one cause. A sex life that was not sufficiently full.

We discussed my sex life. It was not sufficiently full. I asked the analyst how full a sufficiently full sex life would have to be, and the analyst waved a hand airily. "You should have had a hundred and twenty-five affairs by this time." The number seemed staggering and I tried to calculate one hundred and twenty-five on a yearly basis but the dry beach was unable to cope with arithmetic.

"Even so," the analyst told me, "you might still find yourself now with emotional problems. American men are very poor lovers." It occurred to me vaguely that with a hundred and twenty-five of them in my past, poor lovers or otherwise, I might well have emotional problems.

No. No. I wasn't looking at the problem in the right way. " A multitude of affairs is the only solution for the career woman. You had an excellent job and a career worth following. With career women, marriage rarely mixes. The solution is a varied and full sex life."

A wave broke on the beach. I said timidly, "Don't you think that becoming emotionally involved with so many men might in itself cause considerable frustration?" I was pleased with my question. I was in Mars, talking the Martian language knowingly, discussing without shock the Martian point of view. But I had retained, I discovered, the Earth accent.

"There's no need for becoming involved emotionally with any one," the analyst said irritably. "What you mean by emotion is of no concern whatever to your unconscious. Men are more realistic about sex than are women."

A wave rolled in and I suddenly remembered something. "I adopted a foster child in Europe." We discussed this for a few seconds. The analyst thought it nice of me to provide for the care of a child, but the subject was not important. I mustn't detour to side roads. Keep on the highway.

Another wave cascaded. Was I on the highway? "I have a feeling that the maternal instinct is stronger in women than any other instinct. It seems very sensible for nature to have provided women with such a strong instinct for nest building and to have provided men with equally strong sex initiative."

The analyst looked at me bleakly, like a seagull.

The waves were toppling all over the shore. "I can see where sex for the sake of sexual gratification might supply emotional security for a man. But I doubt that it would with most women. Nature seems to have arranged things differently."

The analyst slapped his desk in irritation. "A typical woman's point of view. And it's nonsense, do you hear, nonsense! Women don't understand themselves."

When I left his office I was still trying to divide one hundred and twenty-five men over the years from my physical maturity. I succeeded finally. I stared, astounded at the figure. Having let the dry beach do the arithmetic, my unconscious came in to make a comment on the findings. A wave broke on the shore. Either my unconscious had developed a narrow sense of logic or it had gained a broad sense of humor. That many men a year, the wave had just informed me, would have kept me so busy that I wouldn't have had time for whatever it was that had caused my schizophrenia.

# Sparring Partners

The waves had become increasingly active in the analyst's office. They started rolling all over the beach as soon as I entered the doorway and continued until I exited through the doorway. On the whole, it was a trying experience for me and appeared to be just as trying for the analyst. Whatever else was indicated by the waves, one fact stood out as brightly as a red cape waved by a matador: the waves disagreed violently with the analyst.

I sat through the interviews almost like a third person, a translator of unconscious waves, wondering which of the combatants would win, for the conversations could best be classified as fast sparring matches. Obeying all the rules of surface courtesy, both combatants, nevertheless, managed to sound out the weak points of the opponent and to punch hard and low. Ignoring the waves was something like ignoring Yellowstone geyser; they boiled over in my head furiously, demanding translation. The analyst argued bitterly, more furious than the waves. I left the interviews feeling like the floor of a boxing ring on which two fighters had slashed each other for a dozen rounds, sought the park and stared at the birds. The gulls stared back at me sternly, like church elders, and looked as if they might disapprove of the sufficiently full sex life. The ducks, I noticed, were surprisingly social and had a way of wandering off into the bushes in pairs that was suggestive. The solitary swan glided serenely over the lake, apparently undisturbed by the lack of a mate.

The analyst had urged me frequently to bring him written reports of my dreams. I had explained when he first made this request that I never dreamed, or if I did, that the dreams vanished completely before I awoke. The analyst always looked at me suspiciously when I told him this and implied, not too subtly, that I was holding back on my dreams for fear that they would disclose an interest in the sufficiently full sex life. The night before I paid my last visit to the analyst was a memorable one for I had the first dream of my life. After having been asleep for a short time, I awoke with the dream flashing through my head. I arose, turned on a light, found some paper and hastily wrote an account of the dream, after which I went back to bed and dreamless sleep. The next day I brought the written report to the analyst's office and showed it to him.

"I was sitting in a restaurant," I had written, "talking to my dinner companion, a man whom I had just discovered to be a racketeer. I was very annoyed, not because he was a racketeer, but because I had also discovered that he was a third-rate racketeer."

I was quite elated at having had a dream of any kind, even such a nondescript one as this, and I waited enthusiastically for the interpretation. None came. The analyst rolled his head as if he were going to charge, and then abruptly tightened his lips and started talking about something else.

I had read Freud in my early youth but had forgotten, consciously at least, most of what I had read. It was months after I had left the analyst before I got around to reading Freud again, whereupon I realized the significance of the dream. The interpretation staggered me, for it would appear that unconsciously I had classified all Freudians as racketeers and the analyst as a third-rate racketeer. It occurred to me as being surprisingly coincidental that I should have had my only dream just prior to my last visit to the analyst's office and it occurred to me, also, to wonder if Something had gotten in a last low smack at its sparring partner before parting company.

# The Pictures

When they first appeared, the pictures appeared as if they might be another of Something's parlor tricks and I tightened my hold on my anchor and dug in, reminding myself that Something was a friend and that the Las Vegas incident, however much it had rattled me, had also brought me a lot of money.

The pictures started one morning just as I awoke from sleep and while I was waiting for the alarm to go off. Because I was still sleeping fifteen hours each night I always took the precaution of setting the alarm for the mornings when I had appointments with the analyst—an unnecessary precaution, really, as I always awoke on these days exactly one minute before the alarm went off. The picture was hanging on a wall of the dry beach just as I awoke and continued to hang there clear and sharp for a half-minute or so. An odd picture, a sort of chart drawn on grey paper in ivory ink. There was a large circle and inside the circle, another circle, and inside the second circle, a third circle. Through the circles ran straight lines, radiating from the smallest circle outward. Two mornings later, when I again beat the alarm clock by exactly one minute, the chart was tacked on a wall of the dry beach again. I noticed, this time, that ten lines radiated from the center of the chart to the smallest circle. Two days later I noticed that the second circle had ten divisions for every division in the smallest circle. On its next appearance, I noticed that the largest circle had ten divisions for every division in the second circle. In succeeding appearances, there was nothing left to notice and I only blinked at the chart until it went away.

During the same month in which the chart made its appearances, the dry beach was bombarded with pictures at odd moments. Unlike the chart which hung around sedately like a picture in a museum, these pictures flashed in and out of the dry beach with lightning speed.

As one example, I was walking through a shopping section when a wave broke on the beach reminding me that I had intended buying a bathing suit. I turned into a store, automatically opened my purse, discovered that I had no money on me, and walked out. A picture, clear and in sharp vivid color, flashed on the dry beach, the picture of a long green oblong on whose center was printed in white ink, a large white dollar sign and a large white zero. While the dry beach was blinking at it, another picture zipped in and out — the picture of a blank check. While I was still wondering what all that had been about, another wave cascaded gently on the shore. If I didn't have money with me, the wave reminded me, I did have my checkbook and the store probably would accept it. Yes, I thought, and went back and bought a bathing suit.

The pictures came and went with the same dazzling speed over a month's period and then the phenomena disappeared abruptly. In a way I was somewhat disappointed, feeling that somewhere there was a pot of Las Vegas money under the pictures if I could only find it.

I decided, afterward, that the pictures most probably had not been another odd attachment on Something's machine. Both the waves and Something had been slow of foot and crystal clear in meaning. The pictures, except for the chart which always looked like a note pasted on a door and then forgotten, flashed with lightning speed, not too fast for their senders and receivers, perhaps, but too fast for the dry beach to get more than a swift glimpse. That highly complex piece of mechanism under the dry beach, I finally decided, had a great many units, undoubtedly, working away in separate little departments of their own, doing a great variety of things, keeping a clock synchronized with my alarm clock, remembering appointments, writing a novel, keeping lists of things to buy like groceries and bathing suits; and probably these separate departments had their own system of communicating with each other.

The idea appealed to me. I could see Department $T$ (in charge of keeping time) flashing a picture of the time on its chart at the appointed minute to Department $N$ (in charge of getting the dry beach out of bed and other navigation). A queer clock, I had to admit, although the chart had a so-so resemblance to a stop watch. Then there was Department *L* (in charge of keeping Lists of Things to Get) sending up a picture of bathing suits—this picture not seen by the dry beach—to *N*.

"We're in the shopping section, *N*. How about that bathing suit? I want to get it off my list."

*N*, flashing same picture to Department *W* (in charge of waves): "*W*, please send in one wave regarding bathing suit. We're in shopping section."

*W* sends in wave and then flashes picture of green oblong with white dollar sign and zero. Translation: "I did. Has no money." *N* to *L*, flashing same picture, "Sorry, friend, but you can see how it is."

*L* to *N*, flashing picture of checkbook, "Has checkbook in purse, I think. See what you can do. I'm tired of having that bathing suit on my list."

*N* to *W*, flashing same picture, "*L* insists. Give it a try."

*W* to dry beach, "You have your checkbook, honey. Stores take checks. You know you need that bathing suit."

Maybe some doors had been accidentally left open when they should have been closed. (After all, when you've just converted the motor and installed a half-dozen new attachments, and half the time you don't know what you're doing, you can't get everything right.) The dry beach, I speculated, might have gotten a look at a few flashing telegrams that go on all the time. At least, it was an interesting explanation. The pictures stopped flashing and I forgot about them.

*Part Four*

# The Reasoning Machine

Abnormality departed with a leisurely step. First there was the dry beach, ten days of vacuum. Then the period of the beach and the waves. Then there was Something, that heavy hand of urgent hunches. Then the four- or five-day period when Something demonstrated its frightening and profitable talent for extending. Then the novel-writing days, strangest of all, perhaps, when words from nowhere somehow reached my fingers, ignoring the dry beach altogether. And the pictures, flashing like bright telegrams. The three months of unusual phenomena were as weird in their way as the voices of the Operators. But the anchor remained solidly hooked and, except for a few days when Something seemed to be showing off what it could do in the way of telepathy and precognition if it really tried, I wandered calmly from one stage to another, undisturbed by what was happening, undisturbed by what might lie around the corner.

And then abruptly, overnight, the strange equipment was put away in storage, the regular machinery was hauled onto the dry beach and connected. Reason, as I had known reason, returned. All the old processes were there although it was evident that the machine was moving slowly. And it was evident, too, that as soon as the reasoning machine was installed, the anchor was pulled up and put away. With the return of reasoning came the return of emotion. I awoke one morning, sat down to breakfast, and found myself thinking and feeling. Before I finished one cup of coffee, I was grasping for the first time just what had happened to me and what it had done to my life.

I had been insane. I hadn't had chicken pox, a broken leg, or even a cracked skull. I had been insane, something that was not only a fearful disease, but a stigma. The first assignment I gave the reasoning machine was to determine how much chance there was that people were going to be able to catch up with that fact.

Amazingly, I seemed safe. If I could judge from the letters I was receiving from home—and I was corresponding regularly with seventeen persons—there was not the slightest suspicion anywhere that my trip indicated anything except a desire to break away from my home town and start afresh somewhere else. Also, I had skipped about the country leaving no indications of insanity for anyone to remember. The only blot I could find was the one-night stand I had played in a mental institution, an institution from which, fortunately, I had been able to glibly talk my way out. I had lived in California for months without anyone except the analyst who was treating me, the psychiatrist who had refused me admission to a mental hospital, and the minister who had referred me to the psychiatrist, learning that I was insane. I doubted that either the psychiatrist or the minister was going to do much talking about me and I was relatively certain that the analyst kept his patients' files confidential. Amazingly, I had escaped one of the greatest problems which recovered mental patients have: I did not have to return to a world where anyone knew I had been insane.

My good fortune on this score I skipped over hurriedly. I was concerned, not with my good fortune, but with my problems. I was thousands of miles from the town in which I had lived all my life and where everyone I knew lived; I had quit an excellent job and I was barely capable of doing the routine job I was now doing; I was probably still in need of treatment which I could no longer afford; and I had run out of money and could just about afford my rent on the salary I was making. Fear and worry fell over each other hurrying in to keep me company.

Concern over money prompted me to move to a much less expensive apartment, to discontinue buying anything except food, to eat less, and to stop buying grain for the birds in the park. But, aside from making such simple gestures, I seemed unable to think myself out of my squirrel cage. As the days passed, despite inaction, I found myself worrying less and thinking more, and I was able, after a month, to take stock and to determine in a general way what I could do about such problems as I could see.

High on the list of things to be faced was whether I should return to my home town or stay where I was. Underlying this question was another question: What had caused my schizophrenia, what friction between the dry beach and Something had been resolved in the past in such a way that the mechanism had shattered, and to what degree was I capable of making similarly stupid decisions now, bringing about similarly disastrous results?

The base question was impossible to answer. I still did not know what had caused the split in my mind. I considered the analyst's theory dubiously. To the Freudian, the solution was too simple. All I had to do was get into some bed or other with some man or other (but the men had to be non-Americans—American men were very poor lovers) at very frequent intervals and I would be in no danger of schizophrenia. The treatment seemed impossible to administer unless I moved to Europe, and the theory seemed highly suspect for many reasons, some of them logical ones. Even the analyst had told me that one of schizophrenia's favorite camping grounds was young children. I dismissed the Freudian theory but was unable to replace it with any other. The base question, I finally decided, was impossible to answer for the time being. I would have to take my specific problems, one by one, and make the best decisions I could make.

Should I return home or stay in California? I wanted very much to go home. I wanted to be among friends and around familiar places, safe and secure. I thought wistfully about getting on a plane that night and arriving home the next day. The urge was so strong that I was on my way to phone an airline for information when a thought struck me like a blow. What was I going to do when I got home?

It was completely obvious to me that it would be a while before I was able to undertake the responsibilities of the job I had done. My mind, at the present, simply couldn't cope with it. Also, even though I did not think that signs of my recent insanity were present, indications of it might still be present, as obvious to those who knew me well as it was obvious to me that I could not yet do complex work. The first move Something had made, in insanity, had been to get me away from those who knew me well, a shrewd move in many ways, particularly shrewd if there had been an unconscious purpose to keep my insanity secret. I had been extremely fortunate in being able to hide my insanity from my friends and my family, and I could see only disaster in their gaining such knowledge now. My family would have hysterics in six keys. Friends, at their kindest, reserve a special treatment for those who have been mentally ill. The unkind can enforce a cruelty almost barbaric. I wanted none of either. Either, I was certain, would delay and might even prevent full recovery. Also to be chained with, "She once had a mental breakdown, you know," would give me a horrible handicap in both business and in personal life. No, all things considered, there was no wisdom in returning home for a while. It was sensible to wait until my mind was stronger, until the machine was operating more smoothly.

I was on my way to bed before it occurred to me that my unconscious, that fine friend of mine which had maneuvered me so adroitly in insanity, had maneuvered me, also in insanity, into resigning my job and into writing notes to myself to remember that I must never return to the company for which I had worked.

What was it Nicky had once said? It kept eluding me but I finally got hold of it. "In order to get what he wants done, an Operator has to influence a Thing all the time," Nicky had told me in the early days of the experiment, "and the more Things want their own way, the more resourceful the Operator has to be."

"An Operator's work must be very difficult," I had said.

"Well," Nicky had replied, "once you get to know the Thing's temperament, influencing it isn't too difficult. You learn what appeals to it and what will motivate it most easily."

Good sense! I got into bed, furious. That Something! That busy-bodying, wants-its-own-way, motivating Something! It wants to keep me away from my company, I thought, that's all it does want, and it's down there working the machinery for all it's worth. It's gotten the upper hand.

After two cigarettes I remembered that I had had schizo-phrenia, a split mind, and that until I knew what had caused the split, there might be some point in living with Something on Something's terms.

# The Textbooks

But what had caused my mind to split? Until I found the answer I was going to be under a considerable handicap in charting my life. Which ever choice of roads I made, whatever external emotional atmosphere I chose to surround myself with, whatever internal emotional environment I built up within myself, I was going to find myself wondering at frequent moments: Am I accepting the best parts of life for me—am I making of myself the best things for me—or is there a chance that tomorrow when I awake, I may find Operators standing at my bedside? They had come once without warning and I had been no less rational the night before they appeared than I was at the moment.

What was the mistake I had made somewhere in the past? What monster had I kept under weights in the unconscious? Significantly, it had been a monster that had lain low until it chose to strike. It had preferred, until striking time arrived, the choice of a cage to the alternative of walking around with a mask on its face pretending to be something else (sublimation, the analyst had called such masked monsters, pointing to the novel I had written as a sublimated sex urge). No, this monster had accepted lock, key, and bars until it was large enough to crack the cage and walk giant-size into my mind.

A detail fascinated me. Hook Operating. Yes, there was no doubt about the marked parallel between the maneuvers of McDermott, Gordon, and Boswell and the occupational techniques of The Western Boys. The material from which Something had woven the story of the Hook Operators was obvious. Thinking about this, it occurred to me that there might be wisdom in writing out the activities of the Operators, for in their conversations there might exist clues as to what had disturbed me unconsciously, told in the symbolism of the unconscious.

I bought a ream of paper and plunged in. Unlike schizophrenic patients who recover via shock therapy and whose memories of their hallucinations are blotted from their minds, my memories of the Operators were as clear as crystal. Something (which, along with showing a marked preference for staying in California, also showed a marked liking for putting words on paper) proved to be cooperative, and the conversations of the Operators flowed up onto the dry beach and onto paper with no prodding at all.

I alternated my periods at the typewriter with visits to the library to obtain books about schizophrenia. In no time, I discovered from the textbooks that although the research psychiatrists freely admitted that they were still wandering around foggy bottom in their search for the cause of schizophrenia, all non-research psychiatrists were more than willing to take running jumps into the lake of guesswork.

The reason for the confused status of the research psychiatrists was clear. Schizophrenia, unlike other mental ailments in which the patients show an almost identical pattern of emotional complexes, had a fantastic way of lighting on the heads of totally unlike people; emotional complexes in schizophrenic patients seemed to have no similarity whatever. Also, mystifyingly, the disease occurred among the emotionally well-balanced as frequently as it did among the ill-balanced. Also, it occurred among vast categories of individuals: among extroverts and introverts; among men and women; among people of all racial and national descents; among people of all religious trainings; among people with widely different social and economic environments. It divided its favors with almost determined impartiality among all classifications which the research men could thing of establishing. Only in one area did it display a preference of any kind: most of its victims were between the ages of twenty-two and thirty-two. On the other hand, there was a fair showing of schizophrenic patients who were in their forties, fifties, sixties and seventies, and a good showing among those in their teens and pre-teens.

Psychiatrists usually started their textbook dissertations on schizophrenia in an angry fashion, stating that schizophrenia was the most tantalizing, the most bizarre, the most unknowable of all mental abnormalities, and that its cause was baffling. Why they all went through this routine I'll never understand, because none showed any reluctance in adding his guess as to the cause to the great hodgepodge of guesses that already existed. Some thought it must be the result of unresolved emotional conflicts, even if the particular emotional conflict could not be determined. However, most of them, aghast at the lightning speed with which schizophrenia struck and the indiscriminate way it had of chopping down the seemingly well-balanced along with the obviously not-well-balanced, were equally sure that the cause could not be emotional, but must be organic. Most of these guessed that schizophrenia was the result of toxic substances of some type in the blood, substances probably created as the result of endocrine imbalance. "It's a dysfunction of the pituitary gland," said some. "It's a dysfunction of the thyroid," said others. "Not at all," said a third crowd, "it's a dysfunction of the adrenal."

Concerning therapy, the doctors also had their differences. The only real hope for cure, said some, was to expose the patient to shock therapy at the very outset of the disease and to continue shock until the patient improved. Shock therapy, said others, had no curative effects upon most patients, and the continuous administration of such therapy to patients who did not respond to initial treatments was torturous and possibly harmful. Shock therapy was used over long periods of time, said this latter group, not because anyone expected to cure the patient with the treatment, but because shock quieted the patient, made him easier to handle, and thereby reduced the problems of mental hospital administration. (One of the outstanding administrative problems in mental hospitals is recruiting and retaining low-paid attendants.)

Some psychiatrists were enthusiastic about tranquilizers. The use of tranquilizing drugs had, in some cases, wrought miracles, curing patients within weeks. Tranquilizers, said others, while they were beneficial to patients with deep overwhelming anxieties, had no effect whatever on other patients, and their continuous use on such patients might be dangerous. The wholesale use of tranquilizers in institutions, said such psychiatrists, was merely replacing the wholesale use of shock treatment and was meant only to change the noisy, boisterous, hard-to-handle insane into the quiet, docile, insane—easier to handle, but in no respect saner.

Concerning oral therapy administered by the psychiatrists, I found some interesting material. Most schizophrenic patients resisted oral therapy and stared rigidly through psychiatrists, pretending that they weren't there. But many psychiatrists had noted, among the patients who did talk, an odd ability to throw the doctor off balance by a feat which might have been called mind reading except that the psychiatrists described it as "the schizophrenic's uncanny sensitivity to unverbalized and only partially conscious feelings in the psychiatrist." I read, happily, instance after instance of the same phenomenon described in a great variety of extraordinarily ponderous ways. The one I liked best was, "this sensitivity of the schizophrenic to react to emotional stimuli which are subliminal for the perceptual apparatus of the non-schizophrenic." (Pooh, I thought, it's just a little attachment Something has. When it's screwed onto the machine, Something can extend into the unconscious minds of others. I know what that's all about.) Nevertheless, it was nice to know that other schizophrenics had demonstrated a similar talent. It made the business more normal, at least for us schizophrenics. Anyway, it wasn't witchcraft.

One psychiatrist had taken a few long paragraphs to describe the phenomenon as obtusely as he could: "The schizophrenic, a specialist in the meaning of unreal and inappropriate behavior in his own right, will be only too quick to spot such behavior in others, especially psychiatrists. This aptitude comes from the proximity and easy accessibility which the schizophrenic patient has to his own unconscious impulses and to the primary processes which hold sway in the id, etc." But I liked his summary paragraph, in which he had devoted one comparatively crisp comment to what seemed to be the important point for the doctors. "The schizophrenic," he had concluded warily, "seems to have an uncanny knack for testing relationships with the analyst, for sensing the weak points of the doctor, and this factor imposes certain limitations on therapy."

It certainly sounded as if a considerable number of schizophrenics, with their subconscious minds in control, had turned aside from their own distortions long enough to look into the doctors' subconscious minds and to make a shrewd and embarrassing evaluation of such distortions as they found there. I searched avidly for instances of schizophrenics who had broken the bank at Monte Carlo, but schizophrenics under observation, not too surprisingly, didn't get too near roulette wheels.

Concerning patients who recovered spontaneously from schizophrenia without treatment of any kind, the textbooks had very little to say. Such recoveries had occurred among each of the four classic types of schizophrenia, although they had occurred rarely. In no way did these patients differ from patients who never recovered; they displayed the same delusions and hallucinations to the same degree. But, abruptly, for no known reason, they had snapped out of insanity. Apparently the spontaneous recoveries, occurring as infrequently as they did, had helped in no way to solve the mystery of the disease. They seemed only to add to the mystery of "Why did the individual develop schizophrenia," the equally baffling "Why did the patient recover?"

I came across an intriguing item in an issue of Time. "After more than half a century of brilliant research into the emotional causes of schizophrenia, Zurich's famed psychiatrist, Carl Gustav Jung, made a startling switch last week, conceded that perhaps the cause of schizophrenia should be sought in biochemical poisoning." It was consoling to find that even Dr. Jung concluded that schizophrenia might not be due to emotional upheavals (something one is always ashamed of) and was convinced, instead, that the cause might be toxic in origin, the result of an endocrine dysfunction, a biochemical poisoning (which was more like getting sick from blood poisoning, no particular reflection on you). Consoling, but not very consoling to me. The very material of my hallucinations made it evident that an emotional upheaval had been at the basis of my schizophrenic split. For six months my unconscious mind, when it found its tongue in schizophrenia and made itself heard, had talked unceasingly about the Hook Operators. And for months before the split had taken place, my conscious mind had been concerned about the same thing.

I reread the short article about Dr. Jung and one short statement rang a deep subconscious bell. "Inasmuch as we have been unable to discover any psychologically understandable process to account for the schizophrenic complex, I draw the conclusion that there might be a toxic cause. That is, a physiological change has taken place because the brain cells were subjected to emotional stress beyond their capacity. I suggest that here is an almost unexplored region ready for pioneering research work."

A physiological change taking place because the brain cells were subjected to emotional stress—I remembered something suddenly, and got out the conversations of the Operators and reread them. The meaning of some of the symbolic terms was clear and unmistakable. The meaning of "latticework" (attitudes built up over periods of time to established environments), the meaning of "Operator" (the unconscious mind) and "Thing" (the conscious mind), the meaning of "anchor" (an emotional blanketing, common among the sit-in-the-corner, stare-at-the-wall schizophrenics), the meaning of "Hook Operator." The meaning of "horse" and "bronco." "Horse" and "bronco"? Toxic substances in the blood? I became very curious about the psychiatrists who suspected a relationship between schizophrenia and a dysfunction of the adrenal gland.

# The Bronco

I knew little about the adrenal gland except that it had something to do with the fighting, aggressive instinct in man. I discovered, after some more poking around in the library, that adrenalin was a secretion of the adrenal gland; that the secretion was vital to human life; and that it supplied mankind and a variety of nonhuman forms of animal life with the kind of sudden explosive energy that made it possible, for instance, for a bear to defend itself in an emergency against a mountain lion, and for a man, facing an enemy, to banish fear under a flood of adrenal anger.

The story of the horse and the bronco was what was bothering me and I plodded through the conversations of the Operators again. I had been a natural bronco, the Operators had said, a kicking bronco. Then, an Operator named Burt, mild, calm, conservative, judicial Burt, had changed me into a horse, a well-disciplined, trained horse that bore a load uncomplainingly. The experiment of the Operators, one of the Operators had told me, although it was not being entirely conducted for my benefit, would have one concrete value for me; it would change me back to a bronco.

I mused over my present relationships with people and I had to admit that I had changed considerably from the person I had been prior to schizophrenia. One of the things I particularly didn't like about myself at the present time was that I had become extremely candid about expressing my opinions and considerably more aggressive in rising to and meeting unpleasant situations. I had, for instance, gotten into an argument with the milkman, an argument I would have avoided adroitly a year ago. The milkman was a nasty-tongued individual detested by every tenant in the building; the tenants, however, avoided getting into arguments with the milkman for a very simple reason—the milkman was obviously the kind of acid-tongued debater you couldn't top. One morning he had said something or other to me in his inimitable manner and I calmly, even eagerly, come out into the hall, leaned an elbow against the wall, and gone to town on him. Before I had said one-quarter of what I wanted to say, every tenant on the floor was out in the hall listening, and the milkman, his face a dull red, was backing down the hall, looking as if he would like to throw a few bottles of sour cream at me but, nevertheless, doing and saying nothing. With his departure my neighbors had thanked me and had stood around beaming and beaming and one had asked me in for coffee. At the time the only thing that had annoyed me was that the milkman had escaped before I had finished with him. Afterward, despite my neighbors' congratulations, I had felt quite ashamed of my behavior, had decided that this outburst, so completely unlike me, probably was some kind of aftereffect of schizophrenia, and had resolved to apologize to the milkman.

Two days later, without having had an opportunity to apologize, I had opened the door on my way to work and come upon the milkman browbeating an elderly neighbor who was standing rigidly with her lips pressed together and her face as mad as prunes but unable to get a word in. Calmly, I had leaned the same elbow against the same wall, taken up where I had left off on our first encounter and almost finished before the milkman, not looking red and mad at all this time but just looking as if he wanted to get out fast, had managed to escape. Again I was congratulated by all and again I felt rather cheap. But after that, I noticed, the milkman managed to get in and out of the apartment building before I got out of bed.

On another occasion, this time in the office, when I had been questioned defiantly by a supervisor who obviously liked a certain local politician, as to whether or not I intended voting for him, I had opened my big trap and described neatly how I felt about the politician. I wondered how long I was going to keep my job, and how long it was going to be before the milkman put oxalic acid in my milk.

The bronco was back. Once upon a time, I had been as candid and courageously outspoken, and almost as stupidly tactless. But candor and tactlessness had gotten me nowhere and I had learned to shut my trap, blank my face, and swallow my ire.

The horse and the bronco. The bronco was making a better job of it at the moment, I had to admit. The supervisor, even though she had glared at me, had backed up in her argument and thereafter carefully avoided discussing her politician with me. She had even, thereafter, gone out of her way to do me little favors and to purr at me. I had gained a new respect from the neighbors, who also were purring over me. I had gained a new respect from fellow employees who didn't like the supervisor's political discussions any more than I did, and who were also purring at me. I hardly anticipated that the milkman would start purring at me although I developed a desire to find out if he would and was sorry that he had abruptly revised his schedule so that I couldn't.

The adrenal gland. When you had a healthy active one, one that spurted up quite automatically at times of stress, how did you live with it? (When the bear found himself unexpectedly facing a mountain lion, I learned from the library, the bear's adrenal automatically started spurting violently, making the bear furious. The mountain lion, on such occasions, after getting one snappy look at the bear coming at it spilling its fury all over the place, just as automatically got out of the way as fast as it could.)

If you forcibly, consciously controlled an active adrenal, and refused to permit its secretion from finding its way to your tongue or your fist, what happened? Did the secretion stop secreting? Or did the secretion, not being able to escape into tongue, fist, or hysterics, go somewhere else in your body? In my case, had the detouring adrenalin caused the kind of toxic poisoning which Jung suspected?

The horse and the bronco had been the topic of more than one of the Operators' conversations. The bronco had been converted to a horse by an "operator's mistake" and was being reconverted to a bronco. "This experiment isn't exactly being conducted for your benefit," Nicky had told me, "but one benefit you'll get from it is that it will change you back to a bronco."

If Something, in control of all operations, had constructively applied itself to analyzing the cause of the split and then mending the split (a theory which might be tenable to psychoanalysts who never treated schizophrenics, but which was untenable to the psychiatrists who did treat schizophrenics), then Something had shrewdly reengineered the channels through which the adrenal's flow could escape. I had been led from adjudication to adjudication, fighting the Operators in their own courts. I had been urged to fight and when I had displayed no particular tendency to put my heart into fighting, a band of Operators, the Lumberjacks, had appeared suddenly on the scene to encourage and support me in my fight. Almost forced to fight, I had discovered that fighting paid off. In schizophrenia, the gradual emergence of the bronco was obvious. After my success with the Lumberjacks, I had defied Crame and other ornery Operators and continued with defiance until suddenly the Spider had scalloped out the latticework, after which I had been speedily led to the final adjudication and liberty.

Even the symbolism of the latticework seemed clear. The latticework cultivated in the dry beach by conservative, judicial Burt had been simple: keep your mouth shut and swallow anger. It had been destroyed and replaced with other latticework: sound off, get it out of your system. Unconsciously, it would seem, I always had been aware of the danger of being a docile horse, of rigidly controlling the impulses to kick back. And unconsciously, when opportunity presented itself, I had undone the damage, accomplished something essential, something which in physiological terms might add up to no more than opening the right door for the secretion of an adrenal gland that was spilling its secretion into my blood stream, finding its way to brain cells, and poisoning them.

It made more sense than any theory I had come upon in the textbooks. I was satisfied that I had come upon an answer of sorts, satisfactory to me. But in a way, it was discouraging. I had just about reconciled myself to the fact that I had to live with Something on Something's terms—terms not too difficult to meet, even if they weren't always consciously satisfying. Now it seemed as if I also would have to learn to live with a spurty adrenal gland. It was getting to look as if the dry beach had a lot of compromising ahead of it, on all sides, and for years to come.

# The Psychiatrists and the Schizophrenics

The psychiatrists, recounting their difficulties with schizophrenics, as uncooperative a lot as psychiatrists had found anywhere, had been frustrated by one particularly uncooperative schizophrenic trait. "Schizophrenics," one psychiatrist had said by way of describing this uncooperative habit, "are exceptionally uncommunicative."

I could picture the psychiatrists, sitting down for chats with the schizophrenics and cozily urging them to open up and tell all. The schizophrenics, although occasionally opening up long enough to cozily describe the psychiatrists' own subconscious distortions, usually sat it out, sedate and uncommunicative. Some of them sat and giggled sociably at the doctors; others sat and-looked blankly through the doctors; some, possibly driven desperate by communicative psychiatrists, froze into rigid catatonic statues, sometimes with their hands in front of their eyes, refusing even to admit the presence of the doctors in the room. No matter how you looked at it, the schizophrenics were an uncooperative lot. Except, I saw, that if you looked at it in one particular way, the schizophrenics had achieved anchors of sorts, anchors to which they could hold serenely, impenetrable anchors, immovable anchors, deliberatively fixed so that they would be impenetrable and immovable.

I considered the four textbook types of schizophrenics, so bewilderingly different, so oddly similar. The similarity bothered me more than the differences, because there was something familiar about the similarity, something that rang subconscious bells.

The catatonic schizophrenic seemed to do the most determined job of withdrawal. By some miracle of mind over body, he succeeded in freezing physically into muscular rigidity and remaining frozen in a posture for hours. The textbooks had dozens of pictures of the catatonics, standing immobile in the center of wards, apparently oblivious of the more active patients who bustled about them. They struck odd postures, standing rigidly with an arm extended rigidly or with an arm held rigidly over the head or even with an arm rigidly held before the eyes. Freezing into such postures, the textbooks said, the catatonics would stand for hours, never moving a muscle. No longer wishing to involve himself with living, it seemed, the catatonic had become a statue. A rigid, defiant statue.

The simple schizophrenic achieved a withdrawal which was not as defiant as the catatonic's but just as secure. Like a limp dish rag, he sat in an apathy almost beyond achievement by the normal mind. Sitting silently, staring into space, he showed 'no more awareness of his surroundings than the catatonic, and displayed more ability, really, to escape. There was no need to stand, rigid and defiant against the world, to extend an arm to pinpoint his concentration upon rigid withdrawal, to put up an arm to cover his eyes and to shut out the world, no fear that if he relaxed he might be again sucked into the bedlam of living. His anchor was deeper. His inner eye was closed, just as rigidly as the catatonic's body was locked. Sirens could scream about him, psychiatrists talk at him, attendants bustle about him, without any danger that they would reach the rigidly closed inner core—no matter how hard they tried to penetrate the seemingly receptive, limp-as-wilted-lettuce body. Equilibrium had been achieved at last, internal earthquake and tornado banished, never again to be admitted. He could sit placidly now for the rest of his life in peace. Anchored.

The hebephrenic, on the other hand, moved and sometimes talked. True, movement was mostly restricted to facial expression. At least, to one facial expression. The expression of a clown. The hebephrenic giggled and laughed, smirked and smiled. And sometimes he talked. His words were mostly mumbles, without coordination or sense. His giggling didn't make much sense, either. He giggled and smiled his horrible clownlike smile at everything— the walls of the institution, the nurses, the psychiatrists, other patients. Questioned, he giggled even more. At first sight, the hebephrenic was baffling. Is this what happened to comedians when they became unbalanced, I wondered? But as a group they seemed to have led sordid, cheerless, heavily burdened lives, containing nothing that was worth even a smirk. And there was the hebephrenic's anchor, I saw suddenly. The giggle. He had escaped into a simple pleasant world whose looseness and uncoordination could not burden him with responsibilities, worries and conflicts which were too complex to solve, too fearful to face. He had become anchored in a giggle.

But the catatonic, hebephrenic and simple schizophrenic were second cousins, and I was anxious to learn about the paranoid schizophrenics into whose classification I fit. As a group they were more baffling, more intriguing to the psychiatrists, despite the fact that they communicated considerably more than their second cousins. The paranoid schizophrenic did not communicate to any marked degree, except by comparison with other schizophrenics. But, occasionally he broke down and told the doctors about the Man From Mars who was trying to disintegrate him, or the neighbor in the next apartment who had tried to kill him by sending death-rays through the wall. He would discuss his persecutors quite indignantly, pointing out the complete injustice of the whole business, after which he would occasionally break down a bit more and reveal to the doctors how he was plotting to undo the Man From Mars by spraying him with cold germs when he got him off guard, or how he was inventing a contraption of his own to kill the man in the next apartment before the man in the next apartment could kill him.

I was puzzled by the paranoid schizophrenic when I considered him alongside other schizophrenics who froze into statues, collapsed into apathy, escaped into giggling. If there was one trait that characterized the paranoid, it was his eternal mental busyness.

His mental world bustled with activity and was inhabited with scores of bustling, if imagined, people. Some of his mental inhabitants were a bit odd, such as Martians and death-ray experts; but the paranoid was at least busy with his fancied people, busy at trying to escape his persecutors, busy at finding ways of outmaneuvering them. If his second cousins had turned their faces away from the enemy, the paranoid seemed to have magnified the enemy, the better to look at him. The paranoid, I read, appeared to be constantly conversing mentally with the people in his mental world, fighting with them, arguing with them, challenging them. Yes, I thought, that's just the way it is. And, after a minute, I thought I saw why.

The paranoid's world, once penetrated, was crystal clear in plot; also, it was teeming with attention-compelling color and drama. It was a wide screen movie in which the action was simple, the characters vivid. The Man From Mars might be trying to make dust of him, the death-ray expert might be trying to kill him with invisible rays, the devil might be challenging him to a duel. There was always an enemy threatening, a ghastly enemy, but a ghastly enemy who was easy to comprehend. The easy-to-grasp, solitary-problem world swelled the dry beach, replacing a multitude of unbearably complex and foggily defined problems with which the dry beach could no longer cope. The dramatic vividness of the new enemy intrigued the dry beach, a dry beach that once probably had loved drama and vividness and which now could be hooked with the same entrancing bait. With the new world, so dramatically vivid that it could not be ignored, the paranoid had become alive; and once alive, he had found himself in a world which had something more than dramatic vividness in it. It had, also, a problem. The problem was a simple one, most often that of staying alive by outmaneuvering the enemy. Oddly enough, even though the paranoid was always up against a uniquely powerful, usually superhuman, enemy, the paranoid never was completely frightened or overwhelmed. Regardless of the size of the enemy, the paranoid was in there, giving it a fight.

What was paranoid schizophrenia, I wondered. Just another

anchor, no more and no less, the anchor of a one-problem world filled with the drama and the color that could fix and rivet the paranoid's mind? An anchor to which he could cling happily, busy at what he liked to be busy with, thinking, planning, maneuvering—easy to do, even enjoyable to do, now that the enemy was clearly defined, possible to see, possible to cope with? Or was paranoid schizophrenia more than this? Could it be a type of training attempted by Something for the dry beach? See how easy it is to face up to the enemy, once you can see him—how easy to look straight in his eye, how easy to even spit straight in his eye. And while you're looking and learning to spit, you'll be scalloping out all that latticework of despair, discouragement, unwillingness to face and tackle, learning again to direct an adrenal's flow in the right direction. I sought eagerly to find some indication that the paranoid recovered more frequently than his second cousins, and found that he did not recover more frequently. Paranoid schizophrenia, apparently, was not a way back attempted by Something, or if it were, it was not a way back that was very often successful. And possibly it wasn't even this; possibly it was just another anchor.

Yes, the schizophrenics were an uncooperative lot. There they sat, crowding the mental institutions to bulging point, with more of them coming in every year. To take their places in the psychiatrists' classroom, to listen to psychiatrists attempt to tell them that they could, if they tried, face what they had escaped from; that the enemy had been magnified; that the enemy was easy to face; that it wasn't an enemy at all, really. And all the schizophrenics, the impenetrable schizophrenics, the uncommunicative and uncoop-erative schizophrenics who knew that the enemy wasn't easy to face, that the enemy wouldn't diminish in size at all if one went back and tried to face it again, sitting silent and uncommunicative. And in the same classroom, all the schizophrenics' Somethings who were in charge of the dry beaches now and who knew, as well as the dry beaches knew, that the enemy was not an easy enemy for the individual dry beach; that it was a huge enemy, too huge to face, and one that would still be there waiting if the dry beach went back and tried to face it; and that so long as the enemy was there and the dry beach was as it was, there was no point at all in trying to urge the dry beach to go back and fight. It was better to prop up the dry beach with an anchor, an anchor to be clung to and rested against. Although there were, of course, occasional irresistible temptations to take a few minutes out now and then to remind the doctors that, with their own distortions, they were hardly in a good position to criticize.

I got so angry thinking about the schizophrenics in the institutions that I wished someone would put a checkbook and a Greyhound bus ticket in each of their laps and let them go far, far away from the enemy. Impossible, of course. But I wondered how many of the Somethings, sure that the enemy was behind and would never have to be faced again, would perk up, remove the anchor and let the dry beach take over the president's desk again.

# The Guidance and the Planning

If I were having a slow time tracking down the cause of my schizophrenia, it was clear that once I had unconsciously understood the cause very well. I could cite a spontaneous recovery after six months of continuous hallucinations and delusions, a certificate of sorts, proof that my mind had found the road out of insanity, a feat that is never accidental. If the guideposts that remained in my memory appeared very often to be so much mumbo-jumbo, it seemed at least possible that the appearance of mumbo-jumbo existed because I could not read the strange language. According to the psychoanalyst who treated me, spontaneous recoveries are rare and weird events in advanced schizophrenia and when they occur they present a mysterious spectacle—that of a mind walking out of a fourth dimension into which it has been propelled. The dry beach could take no credit for having found the doorway out of insanity; it had done little except sit on the sidelines and observe. Some part of the mental mechanism that was not the this-is-I dry beach seemingly had known the location of the doorway and patiently plotted a road to it.

No matter how many times I went over the story of the Operators and told myself that it represented only well-organized fantasy without guidance or planning, the clear indications of guidance and planning persisted in standing out.

The guidance was clearer than the planning. I had been maneuvered into a hospital when I unconsciously suspected pneumonia; maneuvered into visiting a doctor when I unconsciously suspected a mastoid; maneuvered to a mountain cabin when I was exhausted from bus traveling; provided with a flashlight so that I wouldn't fall on a dark road; rescued from a mountain lion; maneuvered out of the mountain cabin the morning after the mountain lion incident; reminded punctually of meal times and the necessity for eating; reminded punctually (during the last month) of the need for brushing my teeth and other grooming. Whatever mental level the guidance had come from, it was clearly some level other than the this-is-I dry beach, and it had made certain that the organism was kept in good physical condition while the dry beach was incapable of providing the car.

The planning was almost as obvious. Even on the first day, the voices had sketched in the picture of things to come. This was an experiment, the Operators had told me. My mind was going to be controlled by Operators and I should have to be cooperative for my own sake as well as for theirs. And Nicky had added, as if the success of the experiment were being weighed, I would have one chance in three hundred of escaping the Operators and I would have to be lucky in the bargain. I had been maneuvered away from home, where publicity of my insanity would have made life difficult after sanity had been regained, and where also there existed a company for which I persisted in working and toward which I had developed long established, difficult-to-change attitudes. I had been induced into riding Greyhound buses, where I could sit in schizophrenic apathy while I lived in my mental world, a state of being almost identical on the surface with the usual bus passenger who stares at the landscape, his mind on inner reflections. I had been coaxed into writing letters that would keep the home folk happy, maneuvered to California by the Lumberjacks, figures apparently created for that very purpose, and had been induced to stay in California for the final act. And when the fall of the final curtain was sensed, I had been directed to a minister, to a psychiatrist, and finally to a psycho- analyst.

The guidance was kind and protective and unmistakably clear. The planning seemed to indicate generally that the controlling part of my mind knew what it was doing and had taken many precautions to make sure that no one, including the dry beach, interfered with it until it had arrived at where it was going.

The goal behind the planning? A resuscitation, the Operators had called it. And the conversion from horse to bronco was evident enough. But there was another and more important resuscitation that became clearer and sharper as I reread the Operators' conversations.

IF I CONSIDERED HOOK OPERATING UNSAVORY, WIMP
HAD ASSURED ME, IT WAS ONLY BECAUSE I HAD BEEN REARED AND
CONDITIONED TO THINK OF IT IN THAT WAY.

# Hook Operating

I was intrigued by the subject on which the voices had spent most of their time: the explanation of the Operators' techniques. Some of this time had been spent in explaining the relationship of Operators and Things, the methods by which the unconscious mind exploited and motivated the conscious mind; also, considerable time had been spent in explaining the techniques by which Operators exploited each other. Outstanding among the latter was the weird and unsavory occupation of The Western Boys: hook operating.

In the explanation of hook operating was a clear description of the techniques of some of the people from whom I had run. Nothing to be shocked at, hook operating, Wimp had assured me. Nothing of which Operators had to be ashamed. Hook operating was a business, a perfectly legal business. All Operators played the hook game. The Western Boys differed only in that they made their living at it. And, I had to admit, some of the Operators whom I had left behind me at home had assured their livelihood by such techniques rather than by their ability to do the job they had been hired to do. I had watched men skillfully tear each other to shreds and had been unable to face that fact in sanity without fear and distaste, and in insanity I had gotten another chance to see the same picture and a better opportunity to evaluate it objectively. Hook operating was just a business, just another way of paying the grocery bills. All Operators played hook operating; essentially, it was the technique by which they hooked and motivated their individual Things; and the technique by which they hooked each other. At one point Sharp had said to me, "A Thing can be influenced chiefly because of its desire for money and power. An Operator's security and self-esteem revolve about Operator's points just as a Thing's revolves about money. The hell of it is, Operators and Things are motivated by similar desires. We're both in the soup, Operators and Things alike."

If I considered hook operating unsavory, Wimp had assured me, it was only because I had been reared and conditioned to think of it in that way. And he had added, indignantly, "That Hazel! She's the one who's doing something unethical trying to make you think hook operating is illegal."

"Indoctrination" was one of the words I heard most frequently from the Operators. And patiently, bit by bit, the voices had made their points. I had been led from an appreciation of how Operators worked on Things to a point where I could understand that an Operator might well be expected to approve of hook operating on any level: Operator on Thing; Operator on Operator; Thing on Thing. Something had no objection to hook operating; as competition was the very basis of life, hook operating was an essential technique of living. If the dry beach had learned early in life that the technique was horrible and inhuman and had failed to unlearn the lesson, Something had continued to look at the picture with a shrewder, more realistic eye. This was an important piece of training for the dry beach, the indoctrination into Operators' techniques. It was important for me to be able to look at the Hook Operators whole and straight, without horror and without fear.

# The Doctors

While I was reading the textbooks, I discovered that Something had made its private copy of some of the items which I had read. A few sentences kept jumping into my mind for days afterward. One recurred so frequently that I finally typed it out and contemplated it from time to time. It had occurred in an article by a psychiatrist who had cautiously avoided jumping into the lake of guesswork and who, instead, had stood on the center of a seesaw and observed carefully both sides of all the mysteries of schizophrenia. One of these observations was, "Whether the schizophrenic really creates a dream world intentionally and purposefully, or whether he finds himself in one is debatable."

As cautious comments on schizophrenia went, I considered this one a dilly. It should be clear, I thought, that in schizophrenia it is the dry beach that finds itself in a dream world, and Something which creates the dream. But after a while I thought I saw the reason for the psychiatrist's question. To a psychoanalyst like Dr. Donner, the unconscious mind is an awesome instrument, capable of anything and everything. Unequipped to treat schizophrenics and unfamiliar with psychiatrists' techniques, he had merely carried over his respect for the unconscious mind as an instrument, in his treatment of me. My voices had hinted that recovery was around the corner; the analyst had listened and placed his faith where he had been used to placing it: in the devious language of the unconscious. But to a psychiatrist the unconscious mind, in insanity, is a machine out of working order, no more, no less. But this one psychiatrist apparently had come upon evidences of purposefulness in the schizophrenic's mind. And he had veered from the psychiatrist's usual assumption that the schizophrenic finds himself in an uncontrolled, bizarre and crazy dream to wonder if the dream world might have been created on an unconscious level with intention and purpose.

The reactions of the psychiatrist to whom I appealed for help and the psychoanalyst who helped me are interesting. I told both that my voices had told me that I would be well within two weeks. And the ability of the analyst to recognize the fact that a spontaneous recovery was on its way and the inability of the psychiatrist to recognize the same thing is worth emphasizing. There was a very obvious awareness in my subconscious mind during the days that immediately preceded the cessation of the voices, that the voices would cease, and an apparent awareness that when the voices did cease, the mentality would be in a vacuum for a time and that the organism, consequently, was going to need guidance from somewhere on the outside. It was necessary that the dry beach be parked safely somewhere.

I had been led to a minister who obtained for me (as might have been anticipated) an immediate appointment with one of the supervising psychiatrists in a large mental hospital. I had told the psychiatrist what the voices had told me to tell him, that I would be well within two weeks, and the psychiatrist had dismissed the comment as just another mental aberration, and had told me that I would need care for a long time, and had advised me to get on a plane and return home immediately. His advice (apparently not anticipated) had induced my voice of the moment, Hinton, grimly to order me to a phone book to select another contact. The contact he chose was a psychoanalyst and the choice may have been significant. I related the same story to the analyst. The analyst, more acutely attuned to the purposefulness of the unconscious, much more deeply impressed with its meaningfulness, had sweated out a four-day period waiting for the recovery he believed would occur. On the fourth day, as he was. growing increasingly alarmed by the idea of a mental patient drifting loose about town (an idea which, peculiarly enough, had not disturbed the psychiatrist to any degree) and had started proceedings to have me sent to a private institution, the recovery had taken place.

If the spontaneous recovery had not taken place, the psychoanalyst would have turned me over to some psychiatrist, for schizophrenic patients are not treated by psychoanalysts. The schizophrenic patients belong nowhere on earth except under the jurisdiction of the psychiatrist. All this is as it should be. But there would seem to be missing from the nonanalytic psychiatrist's tools one which the psychoanalyst has often been criticized for having too tight a grip upon.

I had no particular confidence in the analyst who treated me. My unconscious description of him as a third-rate racketeer was undoubtedly unfair. But I think that his values to me were limited. He admitted freely that he had nothing whatever to do with my recovery from major symptoms, and I doubt exceedingly that he had much to do with the fact that I was able to resume normal living shortly afterward. But such values as he had were extremely important to me.

He was able to recognize that a spontaneous recovery was due and to provide what I was unconsciously asking for when I went to the psychiatrist—an anchorage to which I could cling while my mind finished its three-month job of getting the mechanism into normal working condition.

# That Something

What was Something? One of the theories I had come upon in the textbooks was that the schizophrenic split was a physical split of a weird kind, horrible to think about, but intriguing in a way—that in schizophrenia, splinters of the conscious mind split off and hang down in the unconscious. Could this be what I called Something, I wondered, a knowing and purposeful sliver of conscious mind imbedded in the whirling stream of the unconscious, capable of guiding and shaping the extraordinary unconscious talents?

When I thought of instances when Something had displayed considerable resourcefulness, such as the adventure of the mountain lion, I liked very much to think of it as a lonely little conscious splinter hanging precariously in the whirlpool of the unconscious but, nevertheless, holding its own in controlling the whirlpool, and bravely doing the brain work for the family. Harking back to other occasions, such as the train ride to New Orleans when the Drawflies had played The Game for hours, I was quite satisfied to think of Something as the unconscious on a spree. At other odd moments, I confess, I even found myself thinking of Something as a pixie in the garret, or maybe even the spirit of St. Anthony. (During my eventful six months, I had carried with me what I thought was a St. Christopher medal, I was considerably startled, after recovering sanity, to find that the medal bore the figure and name of St. Anthony. At a later time I learned that St. Anthony was known as "the Doctor of the Church.")

I should like to note, at this point, that schizophrenics, long before writers dreamed up science fiction, had—as they still have—a consistent way of developing mental worlds filled with Men From Mars, devils, death-ray experts and other fanciful characters. And while I have found these aberrations dismissed mostly as mental disorders "from which it is difficult to separate the patients, as the hallucinations apparently have some value for such patients," there are a few consistencies about these apparitions which I should like to note."

Regardless of their individuality, they seem to have certain characteristics in common: they are figures of authority who can command with considerable expectation that the dry beach will obey; they are superhuman and beyond the powers of human authorities who might interfere, such as policemen and doctors. Once they appear, the dry beach speedily gets the general drift: either you do what these characters say, or else, for no other human can help you. (I remember that one night I brought up the question of God versus Operators. And after a short pause, the boys brought in Sophisticated to explain the situation to me. Sophisticated being the character he was, I lost track of my original question within a short time. But Sophisticated remained with the subject long enough to explain that Operators, very early in the history of civilization, had surrounded the earth with an airfield of steel rays so powerful that even God couldn't get through. As arguments went, I thought that this was a pretty weak one. But, Sophisticated had pointed out, it was quite plain from the state of the world that the steel rays were undoubtedly keeping God out. And I finally had to admit that Sophisticated had a point.)

Whatever Something was, conscious splinter or unconscious nucleus, it is interesting to conjure up a picture of Something's problems as it gingerly approached the critical moment when the important interior section of the skull was going to be rift asunder.

Something, communicating with its ninety-nine assistants via telegram. Well, you see how it is, boys. We're going to have a mess on our hands at any moment. And there's nobody else but us to undo it. It's clear enough to see what has got to be done. First, we have to reconvert this horse to a bronco. Then we've got to scallop out that latticework. Both were mistakes. I admit it, boys. But, after all, the mistakes were mostly ours, and we'll have to undo the damage. The president's desk obviously can't handle it. And one thing is as clear as the grey in your cells—the damage can't be undone in this damned office environment. The attitudes she's built up to this office are too strong. And you know that if they put her some place and sizzle her with electricity, she'll be out and back here the next month. So, we'll play it safe and hit the road. I always did have a yen to see California so maybe we'll go there. Anyway, it's as far away as you can get without a visa.

Now, the first thing to do—of course, it's standard practice, but it's sound—is to create a superhuman authority whom she'll have to follow. Something that has superhuman power so she won't be running off to a police department or to her cousin Louie for assistance. And we'll make this superhuman authority a little unpleasant. Something she'll be justified in kicking at. Now, that's important. She's a natural bronco but she's lost her taste for fighting anything human. But if we make this image a bastard that's not human, I think we've got a better chance of getting that adrenal working again. But she's got to do it in the right way. We don't want her shooting them, or poisoning their coffee, or stuff like that. You develop that kind of latticework and then you've got another job on your hands scalloping that out. She's got to fight them in court—all perfectly proper and legal. Now, let's see, where are those stable elements. They're around somewhere—oh yes, courts, law, and judges, that's the stuff.

Now, I'll get my writer busy on the script and the dialogue and the characterization. Sam! You've been crying for years that you like to write. Well, here's your chance. We'll need a set of characters and a few million words of dialogue. You got the main idea, Sam ? She's going to have this superhuman authority doing something nasty to her and she's got to learn how to fight them. So, be sure that some of these characters you develop are friendly guys who will give her a hand and help her over the rough spots. That's theme number one.

Now for theme number two. She's got to see that these bastard characters don't have horns and tails. They're just people going about the old crummy business of making a buck in an approved crummy way. That's the way the world is and she's got to learn for once and for all to see things the way they are without going into a tailspin. That's an important part of the conversion and you've got to hit that theme over and over. And be careful of those court trials. The important point is she doesn't definitely win any of them except the last. But she's got to be kidded along into thinking that you're never down until you're out, and there's always a chance to win, if you get in there and give it a fight. After we get that adrenal operating the way it should be operating, that part will be easier. You got the general drift, Sam? Get busy on it. I want Act I on my desk within two hours. And remember, Sam, the dialogue is important. Every word of this is going to be heard.

Now, where are those technicians? Listen, every word of the script is going to be on the air, boys. And it all has to be heard clearly. Now, I want you to fix up a gytex in the rhttymx with a cubdem squared off and then squished. That's for the sound effects. And we may need a little camera work, too, especially at the beginning, so she can see these characters and really get the idea that they're there. Now for that, we'll run a few wires into the rhttymx after you have that set up. And in addition, while you're stringing up all those wires—

It must have been difficult for the director at times, especially when the stage on which the drama was being played ran into unforseen difficulties.

Now, we'll have to get out of this psychiatric ward, boys. Yes, I thought I might go along with some of you and stay here, but frankly, the picture isn't too encouraging. They might cure her and then she'll be right back home in that damned office, and we'll run into the same situation again. And on the other hand, they may not cure her. Frankly, I think we're better off if we scallop the latticework out ourselves. Why? Just plain statistics, that's why. Remember that article we read? Jerry, get it out of the file. Sixty per cent of all schizophrenics are cured or improved by shock therapy. Cured or improved. And you remember how they defined "improved." It meant anything from graduating to the point where you could be trusted with a knife and fork, to the point where you could be trusted outside of a restraining jacket. So, how does that add up, huh? How much have we got to lose, eh? Now the way I figure it, they'll interview observation patients on the first day. Now, when we're in the interview, I'll size up the psychiatrist, figure out what he's looking for and make sure he finds something else. Now, for the interview I'll need that "sensitivity to unverbalized and only partially conscious feelings" gadget. Where is the damned thing? It's supposed to work especially well with psychiatrists and that, in itself, should tell you something, boys.

And then the stage unexpectedly had found itself stalked by a mountain lion.

Now, take it easy, boys. I'm not sure it is a mountain lion although the way it keeps padding along, stepping on the same things we've been stepping on, makes it sound like a cat. Now, don't get nervous. We have that flashlight, haven't we? When we bought it I was just thinking of stuff she might stumble over but it'll come in handy right now. Anyway, it's the only thing we have got. Now, fortunately, we're pretty close to the house that has the yard full of yappy dogs. Now this lion, I think, when it hears those dogs yapping their heads off, will be afraid they're coming for him, and he'll hot foot it. Let's go! Oh, first flash a picture of Nicky. She has confidence in him and she'll go along with almost anything he requests. Have you got Nicky going? Now, get the flash on the dogs. That's it. Listen to them sound off. Fast, now. Flash it on the back of the road. I just want to see—it might be a forest pony or something—it is a cat! Look at the size of that thing. Well, he's not messing around with a gang of dogs. Look at him go! Well, that's that. Is she getting jittery? Have you got that anchor in up to the top? Well, get Nicky to show her those flowers she likes. Have him talk about flowers or something soothing—

Pretty interesting, isn't it, what you can run into in these parts? Now, if she had been in command of operations, she'd have dropped dead on the spot. Gotten so damned rooted in that I'm-afraid-to-move groove she's in, she's lost her touch for handling the unexpected. I'm telling you, boys, before we're through with this business, there'll be quite a few changes made.

# Private Univac

If it was consoling to sometimes think of Something as a shred of conscious mind rather than as a coordinated unconscious, further reading and evaluating made it clear that the unconscious mind, in itself, was as awesome an instrument as the analyst had contended.

Certainly, the unconscious seemed to be able to demonstrate, with ease, some very respectable and impressive qualities. Under hypnosis, individuals frequently demonstrated extraordinary feats of memory. Under hypnosis, many individuals had glibly recited the names of all their classmates as far back as the first grade and even duplicated the formation of their handwriting at the age of five. The unconscious mind seemed perfectly capable of gathering massive volumes of information throughout the years, classifying the information and filing it away in perfect order.

The unconscious, I learned also, was capable of learning without assistance from its conscious partner. I discovered on the popular market a recorder which would teach one a foreign language while sleeping. The individual put the mechanism under his pillow, turned it on, and fell asleep; the next morning he awoke with his conscious mind rested but with knowledge of the chosen language flooding up into it from the unconscious floor.

It occurred to me that most mechanical processes are learned unconsciously. A skilled typist without a typewriter before her is unable to state the location of individual typewriter keys. But if she is seated at a typewriter and blindfolded, her fingers will find the keys speedily and accurately. In the process of learning to type, the unconscious is aware, apparently, that the keys are to be found by fingers guided by itself and so has not burdened the conscious mind with the necessity of remembering the visual picture of the keyboard. Knowing where each key is, the unconscious sends an impulse to each finger as the impulse is required and so performs, with the assistance of the guided fingers, the mechanics of the typing process. The conscious mind has only to think of the words to be typed and the unconscious grabs them quickly, converts them into finger impulses and does the major part of the job of typing.

The unconscious has a similarity to the huge electronic brains which apparently have been patterned on the more obvious abilities of the unconscious mind. Into the electronic brains are fed tapes of detailed information and in the brains is installed machinery for processing the tapes. A question is fed into the electronic brain, the brain receives it, interprets it, refers to its appropriate file to obtain the answer or does the necessary mathematical calculation to arrive at the answer and then clacks the answer out.

What was the batting average of a certain ball player in 1944, the conscious mind of a quiz contestant is asked. If the conscious mind had ever known the answer and ever considered it important enough for the unconscious to label it "keep handy for instant, reference," the unconscious will refer to its files, extract the answer and then shoot the answer upstairs. The more relaxed non-contestant, sitting in front of his television set watching the contestant go into a state of temporary shock, very often can come up with the answer before the contestant. The more relaxed is the unconscious mind, the more easily the unconscious can perform its business. Under the relaxation of hypnosis, it performs its miracles of memory with superb ease.

It was a somewhat startling discovery to me. I had always thought of the unconscious as a whirling pool of repressed emotions, better repressed. Instead, it appeared to be a sort of private Univac, an incredible piece of thinking mechanism, the possession of every conscious mind on earth. The quality of the mechanism differs. The genius has one and the moron has one. But if they vary in ability, they all are equally mysterious. If no one

170

understands the mechanism of the mind of an Einstein, it is equally true that no one understands the mechanism of the mind of a moron. And at best, the marvelous electronic brains can duplicate only a fraction of the abilities of the human mental machine.

But can the unconscious mind think? The analyst had been amused at my query. But thinking about this now, I could see that I had, as do many others, underrated the subtle subconscious machinery. Consider, for instance, a man who owns a business and who is presented with a complex problem, the solution of which will determine whether or not he remains in business. (I watched a friend of mine face this problem over a terrifying ten-day period.) The man searches his mind and searches his mind but can find no satisfactory solution. Finally, he gives up, steels himself to face bankruptcy, collapses in conscious resignation, and then suddenly the perfect solution rises into his mind. ("Of course," said my neighbor on the tenth day of his trial by fire, after he had suddenly arrived at his inspired solution, "of course this is the perfect way to handle the problem. But why didn't it occur to me before. Why? Where was my mind?")

The unconscious, unlike Univac, when it is presented with a problem does more than search its files with lightning fingers. It appears to search and also to consider, evaluate, weigh. First, it must understand the problem. And this it can also do. It can grasp an intricate concept. The conscious mind broods over its problem, and the unconscious, listening to the brooding, grasps the problem.

It searches its files, evaluates, and sends up an answer. The answer is rejected by the conscious mind. The conscious mind broods on the reason for the rejection and the unconscious listens, understands, gets to work again with the new concept and comes up with another answer. Still not good enough? Why? The conscious mind broods again and the unconscious gets to work again, and works until it finds an answer acceptable to the conscious mind. The conscious mind stops brooding and celebrates, and the unconscious rests. For the time being, the organism is out of danger.

Lucky is the man who gets good hunches. Such a Something

doesn't even go through the pretenses of allowing its conscious garret to pretend it can think. The unconscious goes through the thinking processes, arrives at the answer and shoots it up in a geyser of "intuition" or "inspiration." (Women seem satisfied to settle for "intuition," men seem to prefer "inspiration.") The conscious mind of the receiver will make his decision as to whether he will follow his hunch on the basis of his past success with hunches. If the unconscious has been a shrewd thinker in the past, its urges will continue to be obeyed.

This business of hunches particularly interested me. So far as I can recall, hunches had had no place in my mental processes prior to insanity, although in the months which immediately followed my recovery from schizophrenia, the hunch process had been an important tool. Frankly, I think I should have been a nervous wreck if I had had hunches poking me through life. Mine is a cautious temperament which likes to know why it is doing anything before it does it, and which prefers what appears to be consciously controlled, deliberate reasoning to the speedy impact of intuition which comes from who-knows-where and which may lead to who-knows-what. Many temperaments are like mine and such temperaments don't get hunches. The unconscious doesn't waste a technique on a dry beach which won't accept it. All my life when I thought I had been thinking, it may have been possible that the wily unconscious, having thought out the problem at hand, had sent its reasoning and insight upstairs on gentle waves, waiting patiently for the conscious receptacle to say, "Ah yes, if such and such are so, then such and such are also so," at which point it would send up another wave. In the months following my schizophrenia, my unconscious mind may have been operating, with its wave technique, pretty much as it had always operated, except that the processes were more obvious.

The speed with which I had written a novel during the mental vacuum period that followed the cessation of voices had always intrigued me, and I did some research to determine the manner in which professional writers did their chores. I discovered, with some surprise, that most writing appeared to be almost entirely a subconscious chore. A pulp writer, whose creative productions could have been produced very ably, I think, by a simple electronic brain, said in essence, "I never sit down and write until I get a strong urge, because when I do, I don't get anything that's worth anything. It's this way, when I wait until it's ready, it comes out jelled and hot. If I try to force it, it's cold and loose and I have to rewrite it and rewrite it and even then it's never worth much." Other writers who produced work of higher caliber said almost exactly the same thing. "The story wrote itself," was the phrase usually used to describe the birth of some story for which the writer had become best known. Attempting to explain what was happening to them while they were in the flush of creation, writers drew revealing pictures. "I felt like a receiving station for a program coming in." "It flooded my mind like a faucet being turned on." "It would have been impossible not to have written it that way." In a book called The Creative Process, a collection of reports written by talented creative minds, the answer was exactly the same. A. E. Housman, commentating on the writing of one of his verses, said, "Two of the stanzas came into my head just as they are printed, while I was crossing the corner . . . a third stanza came with a little coaxing. One more was needed but it did not come. I had to turn to and compose it myself and that was a laborious business." Amy Lowell reported, "Suddenly words are there and there with an imperious insistence which brooks no delay. They must be written down immediately or an acute suffering comes on, a distress almost physical, which is not relieved until the poem is given right of way." The difference in quality between the products of Housman and Amy Lowell, and a writer of western pulp fiction is considerable, but apparently the techniques of the creative unconscious minds are similar. "All Operators operate," Wimp once told me, "but what you got to understand is that that fact doesn't make all Operators alike. Look at Nicky. He's just a kid and already he's an executive in the Western organization. And look at where I am. You think being able to operate is a big deal because Things can't do it, but it isn't to an Operator. All Operators can operate, but some of them just aren't as smart as others."

The unconscious, so capable of creating literature or pulp fiction, solving business problems, or spurting forth in an inspirational geyser to solve a problem no more important than "What shall we have for dinner tonight?" bulges with mystery to one who watches it with a mechanic's eyes. An awesome instrument. "If it weren't for Operators," Rink had once said, "Things would still be wandering in and out of caves."

But in its infrequently demonstrated "odd talents" the mystery of the unconscious machinery looms as an even greater mystery. There are native tribes in Africa, some of whose members can sense the presence of underground water quite readily. In Africa, at some time, the development of such an ability might have determined whether a race would survive or disappear from the earth. Necessity, at some points in man's progress, may have made it necessary for men to develop odd talents. Perhaps men, in all races, at some time in their history, could sense the presence of underground water. In America today, I learned, there are a handful of such men in the white race who seem to have inherited the odd talent. They are called "water dowsers," and in some quarters they are hired as casually as you might hire a plumber. Grasping the two prongs of a Y-shaped stick in his hand, the water dowser walks along the dry land, searching for a spot where there is a hidden well. He walks slowly until the stick suddenly twitches violently. In that spot, the man who has hired the water dowser digs and finds what he has hired the water dowser to locate, a hidden well of water. Attempting to find some floor upon which to rest a question, one asks, "Why does the stick twitch?" Between the conscious mind and the unconscious mind of the water dowser, there apparently exists an understood signal. A Y-shaped stick, because of its shape, has balance and can be moved violently with little pressure. As the unconscious guides the fingers of the typist, the unconscious of the water dowser apparently guides the fingers that hold the stick. The unconscious, with little effort, seems able to send a nervous impulse so slight that the conscious mind of the dowser is not aware of it, but which is strong enough to twitch the stick violently. So violently that the conscious mind of the dowser has no doubt that this twitch is the twitch he has been waiting for, and not an accidental twitch. This is the signal, strong and clear. He can, with assurance, dig his deep hole, certain that the labors will be rewarded. How the unconscious mind can determine where water is hidden underground remains a mystery. The water dowser who has a clear channel to an unconscious which has inherited an odd talent, cannot persuade his unconscious to reveal how it knows what it knows. He finds water with his forked stick; how he find it, he cannot say.

At Duke University, Dr. J. B. Rhine, who has been researching in the field of extrasensory perceptions for some twenty years, I learned, has demonstrated and classified mysteries which still remain mysteries. He has obtained some remarkable cooperation from the Somethings of thousands of individuals with whom he has experimented, but no information which would explain the maneuvering of the unconscious in its demonstrations. A man sitting in one room with a blank piece of paper in front of him concentrates on the mind of a second man who is sitting in another room visualizing a picture. The mind of the first man will suddenly see the picture which the second man is visualizing and will be able to draw it. He is demonstrating telepathy. One of Dr. Rhine's assistants holds a pack of mechanically shuffled cards, face down. With no knowledge, himself, of the order of the cards in the pack, he asks the testee to guess the symbol on the face of each card before the card is turned over. Some individuals have guessed clairvoyantly, twenty-five times in succession, the correct symbol on the face of the cards. But even after twenty years, Dr. Rhine is still searching to determine how the unconscious mind performs its odd talents. Possibly, conscious man knows so little about the odd talents, that there is no language or concept by which the unconscious can explain its unusual processes.

The more I learned about the abilities of the unconscious, the more willing I was to drop the conscious splinter theory. Something, it would appear, was perfectly capable of getting along without any assistance form the dry beach.

# Mutating Man

The psychiatrists after years of vainly attempting to determine the cause of schizophrenia turned the problem over to the biologists. In the laboratories of the biologists, spiders, fed on flies which in turn had been fed on plasma from the bloodstreams of schizophrenic humans, ceased to spin their orderly webs and began, suddenly, to spin loose, shapeless webs. Other spiders, fed on the blood plasma of the victims of other types of mental disorders, continued to spin their orderly masterpieces.

Experiments of this type have convinced the biologists that schizophrenia, unlike other forms of mental disorders, is a matter of chemistry—that some foreign substance in the schizophrenic's blood splits the mind, disorganizes the personality, makes it as impossible for the schizophrenic human to spin organized human thoughts as it is for the infected spider to spin orderly webs.

What substance? It has not been isolated and identified. No one knows what it is. Only its effects on spiders and other laboratory creatures is known. It is X, a mysterious something which cannot be detected under microscopes but which is there, a powerful something in a schizophrenic's bloodstream.

How did it get into the schizophrenic's blood? Apparently, it was manufactured by the schizophrenic's body. Some biologists think X may be the product of a malfunctioning endocrine gland. Some of these think X may be formed by an adrenal gland, somewhat abnormal from its beginning, behaving even more freakishly in periods of stress. The experiments which indicated that schizophrenia is physical in origin are considered a breakthrough, a firm platform for further research in a defined direction.

But the platform itself is heavy with an ominous question. What is happening to man that such an increasing number of humans should be developing in their blood a substance which splits their minds. The ratio of schizophrenics to non-schizophrenics becomes more alarming each year.

Consider the most extreme of the theories. "I am almost convinced," said one biologist, "that the schizophrenic is an attempt on the part of nature at forming a mutation."

A mutation may take a long time for nature to perfect and in the perfecting there may be many failures. Concerned with life types, the great force of life has only impersonal concern for the individual living organism. Before the first bird with successful wings had been perfected, there were dozens of odd little creatures, unsuccessful experiments, discarded by nature. The number of humans now being born with the capacity for developing strange chemicals in their blood is a startling phenomenon. The biologist who threw up his hands and said, "It is a mutation," at least has statistics on his side,

It is an interesting theory and while I am not particularly inclined to take it seriously, it is worth more than a casual dismissal. Is man now in the process of adapting to an environment too complex or too restricted for his present physical or mental equipment? Is he in the process of becoming something capable of dealing with an environment which is, itself, only beginning to shape and which the force of life is sensing? The first attempts at shaping birds probably produced creatures which looked like poorly adapted lizards. Other lizards, observing their queer cousins, must have shaken their heads sadly and wondered if the world of lizards were falling apart at the seams. I shall prepare man for a changing universe, says the river of life, so that he may be able to live in it. In the process of experimenting to develop new man, I shall make more than one mistake. The first birds were failures but in creating the failures, I learned finally to conquer air.

Consider the parts of man. Man thinks of himself as a mind and a body and is content, for all practical purposes, with this simple analysis. But a human is a complex universe, propelled by a solar system of endocrine glands, a united nation of organs, a vast electronic web of nerves, rivers of blood and masses of specialized cells, some of them specialized for the job of thinking.

Consider the mind of man. The conscious mind with which conscious man identifies himself is possibly the poorest thing man has. Split off from the unconscious in the schism of schizophrenia, it reveals itself as a dry, almost barren, island; the only forms of life on it are tiny, cactus-like plants. I was marooned on it for six months and it is a small place to live. In normal operation, it appears to serve as a sandy beach, a shore for the waves of the unconscious ocean to roll upon.

The unconscious is a wiser part of man but it is still not his nucleus. The unconscious is a private ocean or, if you prefer, a private Univac, a private reasoning machine. It has its job to do in the individual's private world but its job is limited and defined. It does not direct the growth of bone or determine the color of hair. Even the quality of its tides are ruled by a private moon; it does not, for instance, even fix its own intelligence quotient. There is a Director deep inside each human, balancing in its silvery fingers a parcel of genes, a system of endocrine glands, a pattern of organs, the force of life itself. The Director, in turn, takes directions. It is concerned, not only with the individual fleck of life but also with the fashioning of life types. The Directors of the human type may be fashioning a mutation. Or, if you prefer a quieter but equally disturbing theory, they are merely breaking down under the struggle of attempting to cope with factors in man's environment with which they cannot cope.

Consider another form of life, the fly. The fly, in its struggle for existence, encountered DDT. The Directors of flies developed flies which could resist DDT. The new fly is a mutation. The fly was lucky. It found its answer fast. The Directors of the ancestors of birds, endeavoring to develop wings to escape enemies and to obtain better sources of food, needed more time. The wings of birds were an engineering project and a complex one. The mind and body of man are more complex still and the environment with which they must cope is expanding rapidly in some areas, contracting in others, providing, perhaps, the necessity for mutation. What are a few million schizophrenics to nature if a new type is feeling its way to stabilization?

The onslaught of schizophrenia has been rapid, is increasing, is ghastly. If you consider it darkly, it is an indication that man is cracking up. The story of life, on the other hand, indicates that life doesn't crack up quickly. "I am destroying myself with the environment I have created," says man. "You are a small thing," says life, "and you cannot see beyond your nose. I shall shape you to cope with whatever environment you create."

So much for the theory of schizophrenia and mutating man. It is a weird notion but so is a satellite a weird notion. I think, myself, that schizophrenic man is man in the process of cracking up. Having settled with a sort of comfortable gloom into this theory, I remember suddenly some of the dialogue of my Operators. To explain their presence and their actions, the Operators had given me a short but clear explanation. They were conducting an experiment and in the process would make me a freak.

I have forgotten most of the biology I learned, but the unconscious is a storehouse of knowledge and it may have drawn upon consciously forgotten knowledge and mumbled to itself regarding a possibility more clear to it than it was to conscious me. This is an experiment and you are a freak. We are caught in an experiment of mutating nature and you are a sport. We have been challenged by nature and we are setting out to find the answer if we can before the sanatorium walls close in.

It is somewhat deflating at this point, after commending myself for possessing a subconscious which was able to deal successfully with the phenomenon of schizophrenia, to reflect that I may only have possessed a Director and a blood stream which knew a thing or three about dealing with strange chemicals when they appeared. All during those six months when I thought a portion of my mentality and will was fighting it out with madness, it may only be that my Director was busy developing Y in my blood stream to combat X, busy producing a stabilizer to deal with the suddenly revealed instability of a mutating adrenal or pituitary or whatever.

Guinea pig. Freak. How I used to resent the words when the Operators used them. But I take such comfort as I can find in the notion of being part of mutating man. I may be a powerhouse of Y by this time; if you know any unfortunate spiders who have been fed a meal of schizophrenic blood plasma, send them my way and I'll arrange an injection. I have a lot of sympathy for those spiders.

# Hinton: Departmentalized Man

Alone of all the Operators, the curious figure of Hinton succeeded in making me uneasy and uncomfortable.

Perhaps it is peculiar only that the other Operators did not have the same effect, that from the very beginning I was so strangely at ease with them. But from the moment of their appearance I had found myself judging them for their human rather than their superhuman qualities and having toward each of them much the same reactions I might have had, had I been sane and they real. I had liked almost all of them and some of them I had liked very much. Some of them I had liked less. The bullying Crame and the sadistic Jocko had annoyed me and the vicious Dorraine had frightened me. But only with Hinton had I been uneasy, uncomfortable.

Certainly, Hinton's appearance would never have inspired a relaxed feeling in anyone. His cavernous face and lean body seemed to be less, rather than more, than human. His too-long lank black hair screamed defiance of a social order that accepted barbers as a cornerstone. The stillness of his body and the quiet brooding of his face might just as easily, I should think, have brought a measure of relief to a six-month situation in which a half dozen grey wraiths usually were moving busily over the scene and a half dozen voices were talking, talking, talking. But there had been no relief in Hinton.

He had been around almost all the time but always quietly around, standing in far corners of rooms, looking at me out of the corners of his eyes, or sprawled with such relaxation that he seemed broken, in the most comfortable chair. While the other Operators chattered with me, the silent, brooding Hinton observed me. If I occasionally took time out to study an Operator, I rarely had the impression that any of them was taking time out to study me. But Hinton was always studying me. It was no great shock to find at the end, when other Operators had disappeared, that Hinton was still on the scene. He had the persistence of the silent.

At my bedside that first morning, there were three shapes. There was Burt who, the Operators told me, had been operating me recently. White haired, sober faced, quietly impressive, Burt might have just stepped down from a Supreme Court bench. There was the weird looking Hinton who, the Operators told me, had operated me years before. There was Nicky the pleasant, well-mannered, sympathetic youngster.

The first thing an Operator said to me was said by Burt. "It is necessary for the good of all concerned," Burt said, "that you get to know Hinton better." Burt seemed to have made an appearance for little else than to perform the introduction, for shortly afterward Hinton informed him that he was being discarded. Nicky was obviously upset at the news and just as obviously could do nothing. Hinton appeared to be in control.

How many parts of yourself do you bury in the process of maturing, adjusting to society. Half-bury? Quarter-bury? Departmentalize?

Once, according to the Operators, or if you prefer, my talking unconscious, part of me, a part symbolized by the non-conformist image of Hinton had been in control. Afterward, part of me that was symbolized by the image of conformist Burt had seized control. Burt had grown big and Hinton had become small and I had become, in the process, an adult. In many individuals there is something like a Hinton half-buried, quarter-buried, or channeled into restricted areas.

The unconscious is a Univac-type machine, let us say, and in normal operation, it responds to tape feeding from the conscious mind. There is, suddenly, a breakdown in the machinery. The conscious mind cracks or is invaded by strange chemicals. The great latticework of electronic wires that connect the conscious and unconscious are closed down hurriedly and the unconscious surveys the wreckage. There has been a tragedy in a miniature planet. The unconscious units confer with each other in quick horror. What shall we do, say the units. What in hell has the Director of our world been up to that this should have happened to us? If we are to survive, we must take action.

For adulthood, Burt had had his purposes. For the task of curing insanity, he was judged useless. He was dropped. Where would Burt have brought me? To a mental institution, without a doubt. Coincidentally, I actually got to a mental institution within a few hours after the Operators appeared. The symbols of Hinton and Sharp got me out. While I was in the institution, I had strange dreams which the Operators called Black-Out movies. In the movies, an unseen artist painted a portrait of Burt with horns. It was a child's picture painted with a child's malice. It was a personal, malicious, picture and I remember thinking at the time that Hinton must have been the unseen artist. It was obvious even to the dry beach that to a Hinton, a Burt would be a villain. The portrait painting in the Black-Out movies is interesting when compared with the apparitions of the Operators that moved before my eyes every day. The apparitions were impersonal, sharply symbolic figures drawn by a more objective hand.

"A non-conformist," said the maker of hallucinations, drawing the picture of Hinton. "A conformist," said the symbol maker, drawing a picture of Burt. "A pleasant, likable child," said the symbol maker, drawing Nicky, "Sharp, quick, alert," said the symbol maker, drawing Sharp. Behind the units of the unconscious there appeared to be a wholeness, a Manager of sorts, selecting for its job of curing insanity, its choice of machine parts. For the job at hand, or at least for the job of getting the journey under way, Hinton, Nicky, Sharp.

Assuming the manager and the choice, why these parts of a mentality for a job of this type? If you saw the shape of Hinton, you would know that this was the cat who walked alone, who did things his own way. If you looked at Nicky, you would see that this was an agreeable, pleasant, individual who could be trusted in contacts with people to be quiet, pleasant, agreeable. If you were to see the figure of Sharp, you would know that he was quick and alert, one who could maneuver his way out of awkward situations were such situations to develop. If you had a six month journey before you and these three were to be your guides, you could guess to some degree what your journey was going to be like.

Insane, I traveled around the country for months, meeting many people, doing many things which have not been recorded here. This is not the journal of a sightseeing trip. If anyone suspected that I was insane, there was no indication of it. In California, insane, I visited a physician regularly for an assortment of minor ailments. If he saw any indications of insanity in me, he did a remarkable job of camouflaging it. Nicky, the pleasant, and Sharp, the sharp. Considering the journey, these two choices were obvious. These two made it easy for me.

But why Hinton, the nonconformist, the odd cat? Why not Burt the sober, the conservative, the judicial. With safe, solid, Burt in charge, the best I would have gotten was a sanitorium. I might have recovered in a sanitorium, even surrounded by female wrestlers who became annoyed with me for frustrating them. If you are going to recover from schizophrenia, it may be that you will recover anywhere. I would have returned, without a doubt, to the environment I had left and with which I had failed suddenly to make an adjustment. Burt was discarded. Hinton was placed in charge.

What did Hinton represent in the land of unconscious symbols? A portion of mind that was prominent in childhood and which had been buried partly in adulthood? I was, like all children, no conformist. And like most people, I grew up to be the model of conformist adult. The only difference I can see between myself and most people is that in the process of maturing I learned early to live separately in different departments. I became, in my early teens, a departmentalized child. It is not necessary to sketch the history of my childhood here but it is necessary to draw in some broad lines. I was an ordinary enough child but I had some oddities. Because I was also a gregarious, adaptable child, eager to become an accepted part of my community, the oddities learned early to manifest themselves in safe places. My oddities manifested themselves, in my early teens, in mathematics and English composition classes.

I was a top student in mathematics and English composition but both math and English teachers considered me an oddity. In high school, I never solved geometry and trig problems the way other students solved them. But, always, I got the right answers. I have forgotten almost everything I knew about math but what remains in my memory is the picture of going to the blackboard day after day to draw the strange figures by which I had solved ordinary problems. At first the teacher surveyed me curiously. Had I, after having solved the problem in an orthodox way, fooled around with it until I had finally come upon an unorthodox way? No, this was the only way that had occurred to me to solve the problem. After a while, the teachers tolerated me and even, occasionally, showed me off. I gained a certain reputation among students. It is something to devise solutions in mathematics which even the teachers haven't come upon. I was not criticized for being odd. It was a safe department in which to be different.

In the field of English composition, I got off to a more precarious start. I lived in a community where to be different was to be suspect, where the lines of thought and behavior were rigid. In my freshman year in high school, there was a short story contest open to all students. It was not expected that a freshman would win it and my story brought me instantly to the attention of the school administrative staff. The judges of the contest were individuals from outside the community and they had awarded my story the prize as much for the theme as for the writing. "An unusual theme for a child," said the judges. The school staff thought so, too. A battalion of teachers, a vice principal and a principal interviewed me. Where had I gotten such a strange theme?

Strange? It seemed perfectly ordinary to me. In the story, a child of thirteen—my own age at the time—comes to the conclusion that there is no God as the picture of God is shaped by religious training. Having come to her conclusion, the child decides to close the door upon any concept of God and to shape her thinking and her living as if there were no God. In a biology class, she comes up against the laws and rules of nature, with sharp shock. There is design and pattern in nature. It is apparent in a grape, a bird that plucks it and sprinkles the seeds about, in the earth that receives and nourishes the seeds, in the rain that nourishes the soil. The design is large and impressive and the pattern too big to be composed by anything smaller than a God. The concept of God is restored, in a different form, but restored.

I went through a succession of interviews with adults who looked at me curiously. Where had I gotten such a theme? Why, I told them, it had happened to me and so I wrote it. If the teachers of the school had been awarding the prize, I doubt that I would have received it. Children of thirteen, in that community, were not supposed to think that way. The teachers poked their anxious, inquisitive faces at me and I could feel their uneasiness oozing from them. One teacher, in charge of the school newspaper, rescued me and put me on the newspaper staff. I continued to write my odd stories for the paper. In English composition classes I became, quickly, a pet. I had somewhat odd ideas but I was creative and coherent and could be depended upon to place in inter-high-school essay competitions. Hinton had found another department in which he could safely expand.

I attended a small college, snobbish in attitudes, rigid in thinking. My experiences in college paralleled my experiences in high school. It was all right to be different, so long as you were different in safe areas.

As an adult, I continued to live in the same community in which I had been reared. It was, in some ways, a colorful community, but at its base it was staid and rigid. Hinton, from necessity, grew small and Burt grew large. At my core I was gregarious, adaptable. Burt was my means of adapting, fitting to the community. Hinton stayed with me but was buttoned up in Burt's pocket. I worked as a technician, and answers in my field of work were somewhat difficult to come upon. I learned early that if I wanted results, I would have to devise new methods. I had learned much earlier that it is wise to keep unusual methods to yourself. The people I worked for, fortunately, had little concern with methods so long as I got results, but I was careful to display only results, not methods. In that community, to gain a reputation for being different, even in work methods would have brought about some degree of disaster. I had a sure, perceptive, instinct concerning how different I could be in any situation.

In my social life, I was a Burt. Here was an area where it just wasn't possible to departmentalize Hinton. Early, I adopted attitudes that fit into the community rules and patterns of behavior. I became the very model of a Burt. A Burt is solid. It puts down roots that are strong. It has a defined and understandable shape. It can be trusted. Its rigidity and inflexibility are its assets.

As a young adult, I dug into the community, living by its codes. You went to work for a company and you stayed with the same company until you married or became pregnant or died. You advanced in the company, step by step, until you reached your top level. You didn't flit around from job to job. You were expected to adjust to your company as you adjusted to the community. At my company, I adjusted well until I came up against something, suddenly, which Burt couldn't handle. Hinton might have been able to cope with it but Hinton had long been restricted to a limited area, work methods. He was never permitted out of Burt's pocket for any other task. The human Hook Operators appeared and started their operations and Burt could only behave like a Burt. Overcome by fear, he could neither fight nor run. He could only stand, digging in, until tragedy struck.

In insanity, there is nothing more important than escape. The individual, whether he is invaded by strange chemicals or not invaded by strange chemicals, is caught in a situation which says plainly: fight or run. The individual who is to become schizophrenic can do neither. He hangs on, digs in, breaks finally, unable to meet stress. What is stress? Stress is a situation which you have not learned to meet and which terrifies you, occurring in a place you cannot leave.

The Hook Operators were new in my life when they appeared in Knox. They represented a type of human behavior that horrified me because it was so new and vicious, and which paralyzed me because I had no idea whatever of how to deal with it. The behavior patterns of the people I had known all my life were fundamentally decent patterns formed from principles and codes that had been built into individuals. Coming upon the Hook Operators suddenly was something like turning a calm winding country road and finding myself in a nightmarish jungle. I had had no training for journeying through jungles. The tigers terrified me but the country road was the same country road I had traveled on all my life and it never occurred to me to turn and run. I could only stay and shiver before the teeth of the tiger.

But, it is obvious, other people in my environment, faced by the same tigers, didn't break, and I doubt that many of them had more experience with the Hook Operators than I had had. I suppose that what I am saying is that I broke because I had become too rigid, too departmentalized, too well shaped and fitted to the community as I saw it. I think I recovered, also, because I was departmentalized, because one of the departments, represented by Hinton, was able at the critical moment to rise, take over, and become the ruling department. I did nothing that was essentially new in resurrecting Hinton and changing overnight from a conservative, rigid personality to someone who galloped off in Greyhound buses to cure insanity. I was only departmentalizing to meet a situation, something I had done all my life.

Why couldn't I shift gears and re-departmentalize on home ground? If I could have convinced myself, consciously or unconsciously, that Hinton would have been acceptable on my home ground, I might have shifted departments successfully without becoming schizophrenic. The difficulty was that Hinton, to my way of thinking, would have been even less acceptable in that community than the Hook Operators.

The largest part of my hallucinations were concerned with learning the ways of the Hook Operators and learning how to fight them. Insanity was, for me, a training program, accompanied by escape from actual stress until I could gain what I needed psychologically to face the same stress in actuality. What was self-cure? A manager of sorts inside me, far wiser than I consciously was, appeared to be aware of the cause of the schism and possessed of a knowledge of how to mend the crack. "It is necessary," the manager seemed to be saying, "to get away from an environment to which too good an adjustment was made and which changed overnight to a new environment. We shall discard the environment and with it, the attitudes and rigidity of personality which the environment enforced. At her base, this individual is adaptable and the process of self-cure is obvious. We must escape from a rigid environment in which a jungle has developed to a free environment, even though a jungle may exist there, also. In a free environment, Burt will not be necessary and the dangers he carries with him need not be feared. We shall kill off Burt and replace him with Hinton, something which cannot be done in this community by this particular human being. Others, less rigidly departmentalized, may make the change with safety. This human being has made an adjustment to her community which doesn't permit dealing with the community and the Hook Operators at the same time. Of primary importance is escape from the community."

There are many non-rigid communities in America but it is probable that the one to which I went on a Greyhound bus, directed by the Operators, was the one best known to me for its quality of non-rigidity. I arrived there finally, settled down there finally, and readjusted finally, becoming in the process, a considerably different person with Hinton larger, Burt smaller. No institution could have done more for me. In all probability an institution would have aimed at shaping me to return to my community and would have failed.

It is interesting to note that when I left my apartment that first morning, Hinton insisted that I bring along my portable typewriter. Why a typewriter, I wanted to know? I used it rarely and it was a heavy article to carry. But because Hinton insisted, I brought it along. It was one of Hinton's tools and one for which he undoubtedly had plans even on that first morning. I never opened the typewriter during my journey until I opened it at the encouragement of an analyst to write for therapeutic reasons. It played some part in my recovery and a considerably larger part in the writing jobs I was to get. At the very outset of insanity, it would seem, plans were being made for a new sanity. The new environment had been chosen, the road plotted, the recovery hoped for, the new life already in focus. The Operators may have had luck but there is evidence, also, that from the very beginning they had some idea of what they were doing.

Consider my spider web. The dry beach of my conscious mind had nothing to do with the spinning, would never have been able in its Burt-rigidity, to spin as well. It sat, in insanity, looking into the cellar, watching the fascinating spider. A part of my mental mechanism had remained sane, had made plans and had planned fairly wisely.

Looked at in a certain light, there was much in my prior sanity which was not particularly stupid. Individuals adjust, if they are adaptable, to the mold of the community of which they are a part. In adjusting by departmentalizing, I made a cautious, even cowardly, but not unintelligent adjustment to the community of which I was a part, considering the elements I had in me. I succeeded in adjusting well. There may have been certain qualities in my temperament and mentality which might have made a happier adjustment to another community but I accepted the community and instinctively did what I could with it. I used, for all I was worth, the qualities that were acceptable in the community and departmentalized what was not acceptable to areas where they could fit and would be accepted.

I seem to be blaming my community for a personal tragedy. I am not. There was nothing particularly wrong with it and there was a great deal in it that was right. It was a civilized community. The tragedy was that, over night, certain jungle qualities appeared faster than I could adjust to them. The error lay, not in the community in which I was reared but in the way in which I, as an individual, adapted to it. I departmentalized, burying elements inside of me which should never have been buried and as a consequence lost wholeness to gain acceptance for a part of me. Had I had the courage to be myself, I certainly would never have been called neurotic but at the worst, different. But 'different' is a criticism and one to which I had become extremely sensitive.

Losing wholeness to gain acceptance for a part is, I think, the tragedy of the schizophrenic. He cannot be himself and ask his environment to accept him. He tucks away, whether he does it in neat boxes or in sloppily wrapped packages, secret worlds of himself which he cannot bring himself and his environment to face. He may, without self discipline, live in a world of fantasy to compensate or he may, with more self discipline, kill parts of himself or squeeze parts of himself into rigidly confined areas.

Regardless of his method of making his adjustment, he is guilty of self murder and must, as a consequence, live with a lively corpse. He may, if he is fairly well organized mentally, succeed in keeping his corpse in a locked coffin, allowing it liberty at chosen moments. In any case, he is a determined conformist, conforming because he is a coward. The corpse may rebel and lead him slowly into areas of fantasy where it can dance a jig; or it may cooperate and lead him into rigid departmentalization. If the result is the latter, he is safe only for so long as the pattern of his life remains as rigid as he is; when it changes, the departments fall apart.

Once a schizophrenic, always a schizophrenic, the psychiatrists used to say. They did not mean that the schizophrenic is doomed to a lifetime in a sanitorium but that the potential weakness is in the personality makeup. It is not that the schizophrenic is an individual who has become a misfit. On the surface, he fits too well. It is that he has never learned the job of fitting his whole self. He has learned only to divide, separate.

It is three years now since the Operators left me and I have gone through a series of shifting gears, adapting and trying out new assortments of departments. "Has my head been damaged so it can't be shut?" I once asked an Operator and received a sympathetic answer. "Frankly, I think it has been. However, it's nothing to worry about. Heads can always be mended by one process or another." The new departments are well suited to my new environments and better suited to me, but they are still departments and I live separately in them. I have mended my head and myself but it is a patch job. Whether the initial cause of my schism was physical, a matter of a slightly different adrenal or pituitary gland, or psychological, or social, or some combination of all these, the solution I found for my schism was the same solution I found early in my life for living. I separate. The fact that I feel considerably more solid than I ever felt before in my life is some consolation, but a patch is a patch and there is no point in calling it anything else. The specter of the critical community eye still hangs over me, and if I ever find wholeness, it will only be when I finally find the courage to look back at it without fear.

Where no man knows the answer, anyone has the privilege of making a guess. My guess is that the individual who is to become schizophrenic is as I have described him—an individual without adequate courage who learns to separate himself so that he is acceptable to himself and his environment. I suspect that the strange chemical in his blood stream is a result, not the cause, of the schism. I suspect that sooner or later in his life the separated individual meets unbearable stress and under the stress some part of his endocrine system—and in the overcautious, fearful schizo the adrenal seems to be the most likely villain—starts pouring out its secretion to meet the stress and that the secretion, dammed, forms X and that X in turn splits the mind. In my conflicts with the Operators, I suspect that I was not manufacturing Y, but learning how to recondition an adrenal gland so that the free natural flow of its secretion could wash away X from my system.

# Memo on Mental Institutions

Taking a holiday from the textbooks one evening, I picked up a book whose title seemed to indicate that it might be escape fiction. But, almost as if I were pursued by a one-track fate, I discovered as soon as I opened Joseph Kramm's *The Shrike* that it was not a play about a haunted house but was, instead, an excellent play about a man who is admitted into a mental ward of a city hospital for observation and who, despite his considerable sanity, has considerable difficulty in getting out.

"Easy to get into, difficult to get out," says Mr. Kramm of mental institutions, and while this is not the main issue of his play, it is an issue around which the action of his play revolves. I gathered that the horror of the situation presented by Mr. Kramm in his play had a tremendous impact on audiences and I can well imagine that, had I read the play before my adventures in schizophrenia, I might have had the reaction which Mr. Kramm sought. However, I read it too late. I had a hilarious five minutes when I put the book down, remembering how difficult it had been for me, cuckoo as a cuckoo clock, to get into the mental institution to which I appealed in the last month of my insanity, or to stay in the one to which I paid a fleeting visit in the first month.

I had no wish to stay in the psychiatric ward when I was taken in for observation but neither has anyone, I would guess, who has breathed the freedom of insanity. But the ward was too easy to leave. I have only sympathy for the psychiatrist who dismissed me. The operators of the insane are wily and they gave me all the right answers to the questions the psychiatrist asked. It may be, as Mr. Kramm points out in his play, that psychiatrists prick rather than probe with their questions. There is an old story about a motorist whose car broke down close to an asylum and who was told how to patch it together by three of the mental patients who were leaning against the wire fence that surrounded the institution. The driver was startled when he realized that the ingenious suggestions had come from mental patients. And the patients were perceptive enough to understand how he felt. "What you must remember," one of the patients told him with a grin, "is that we're here because we're nuts, not because we're stupid." The psychiatrist takes such a hazy view of the schizophrenic's unconscious intelligence and perceptivity that his standardized questions make him a pushover for the blank face and the wily mind that is concentrating on outmaneuvering him. However, I assume that I would have been retained in the hospital had the psychiatrist suspected that I was mentally ill.

However, it is difficult for me to gauge what went on in the mind and heart of the psychiatrist in the institution to which the minister referred me. The institution has a good reputation and the psychiatrist had an important position in it. He most certainly knew that I was insane and he knew that I was alone in a strange city. I can still hear the casual coolness with which he informed me that I could not be admitted inasmuch as I had not lived for a year in the county in which the hospital was located, that I seemed to be well controlled, that it would be advisable for me to get on a plane and go back to my home state—and I assume, perhaps un- fairly, that he was primarily concerned, as a county employee, that I should not stay there and add to the local tax burden. I also recall the casual coolness with which he extracted ten dollars from me for this piece of advice and casually, coolly, lifted his jacket and slid it into his left trouser pocket.

Perhaps you have seen or read Mr. Kramm's play and carried away from it a haunting fear that someday you may find yourself in the position of his hero, unjustly committed to an asylum and almost despairing of getting out. It would appear that you have little to worry about. And if you have in your family someone who may become mentally ill and who may take it into his head to wander around the country, you can at least console yourself that he may wander into an institution in his home state.

A great deal has been written about the conditions of mental hospitals and, for all I know, there is still a great deal that should be written on the subject. My story of mental institutions is short. I couldn't get into one.

# The Knife and the Hatchet

I was in the receptionist's job about three weeks when it occurred to me that Southern California offered a better-than-average job market and that I had a fair chance of getting a better paying position. It was almost exactly four months after the day on which my voices had vanished that I bought a newspaper and found myself staring at an advertisement which said "Writers Wanted." I remembered the kind words the analyst had mumbled about my novel, decided that it might be best if I postponed returning to my technical work, and blithely made an appointment for an interview. I was hired. The employer's only comment was that my technical experience indicated that I had an orderly mind.

The value of an orderly mind in the job to which I was assigned is debatable. The industry was a somewhat unusual one and the department in which I worked was unusual, even for the industry. The work, generally, fell in the field of publicity, and the office was inhabited by some of the strongest and most extraordinary personalities I have ever met.

Adjusting to the job proved to be easier than I had anticipated despite the fact that the job proved to be considerably more complex than I had anticipated. But after a month I was able to get my head out of my blotter and take stock of what lay around me. A few days of taking stock showed me clearly that, despite the unfamiliarity of the work, there was something about the office that was horribly familiar.

B wanted A's job. C and D were planning to make a dash for B's job as soon as B had successfully demolished A; both helped B in his program, joining forces that would obviously last only until such time as they found it necessary to demolish each other. E wanted to step into C's job as soon as C got B's job, and concentrated on destroying both D and A. F also wanted C's job and was doing her best to hatchet A, D, and E. There was a G who had his eye on D's job and who was doing as nifty a slander job on

*C* as I've ever heard. Then there was an *H* who wanted *F*'s job and who did his best to destroy *E*. (You must remember, Barbara, all offices are like that. You've just got to adjust to the situation; you've got to learn to live with it.) I didn't know how long I was going to live with it, but I felt inclined to look at it. Dear God, I wondered, are all people in business like this? I never seemed to run into such characters among my personal friends, but they turned up in offices like rank reeds.

One thing was certain. This tribe could have given cards and spades to the boys at home and still finished with the pot. They had a certain resemblance to the Operators in Schizophrenia-land which the employees in my former company had never had—they accepted what they were doing as a way of life, with no time lost in justifying their actions. The speed and nonchalance with which they slit the handiest throat riveted my stunned attention. I had blundered onto a scene where the shelves were loaded with the sharpest instruments in the rack and where hesitancy in picking them up was displayed only while someone decided which edge was best suited to the particular situation. I hastily counted the few months which separated me from insanity, wondered if I shouldn't play it safe and quit, and decided that it was now or never. Something had done its best for me. The least I could do was take the postgraduate course on my own.

I occasionally ran from the scene, nauseated, but came back doggedly. If the ground beneath my feet was rocky, it was ironically fortunate that I had developed the skills for crawling over the rocks in insanity. The Operators, before they had returned me to sanity, had destroyed the material out of which insanity had been born. The latticework had been scalloped out and regrown. The old attitudes and patterns of thinking and points of view were gone; they had been replaced with a knowledge of the techniques of operating.

One fact stood out clearly. There was no way of protecting yourself from these hatchetmen except by picking up a sharper hatchet and learning how to use it. I told myself, somewhat smugly, that I could never wield a small knife, let alone a hatchet. Then, I realized with a shock that I was absorbing the fine points of the hatchetmen's techniques; and that if I weren't yet using the techniques, I was unconsciously building up the skills rapidly. I found myself watching the intrigues of my companions and planning the best moves for each in turn. I knew, before I reached the next corner, that the next step in my learning program waited for me around that corner—the ability to rationalize that anything I might do to these individuals would be richly deserved, after which I could plunge in.

New and at the bottom of the ladder, I was almost totally ignored as a target for the knife and hatchet. I wasn't of a size worth cutting up. By way of self-protection, I tried two small maneuvers. I carefully retrained my accent to one I had picked up in a small college some years before. Its values were obvious. I made neither a good audience nor a good conversationalist. No one was ever certain of what I was saying and as a consequence I made an elusive target. I also had some luck in bragging about the strength of some abilities I didn't have and bemoaning my lack of efficiency in certain fields in which I was quite good. The knife was almost immediately thrown at an area in which I could hold my own, and I avoided getting the knife in areas where it might have been effective.

I looked carefully at the scene and studied it. A year later, when I became eligible for bigger and better jobs, I took an even closer look. I had resisted putting into practice a dozen maneuvers sharpened by Something before they had been plopped into my conscious mind. Without too much effort, I saw, I might become a fairly efficient Hook Operator. I had had to learn to live with Something and I had had to learn to live with a spouty adrenal; I discovered now that I also had to learn to live with the dry beach and I was somewhat surprised, this time, to make the discovery.

I was not at all concerned with what I might do to the individuals around me in the process of cutting them up. Nor was I any longer afraid of being knifed. But I was concerned with what would happen to me in the process of becoming an expert at swinging the hatchet, clutching and fondling the knife. The litany which reads, "Face your environment, refuse to run away from it, adjust to it, face its battles realistically," is so much hooey as far as I'm concerned. You adjust to nothing without changing your shape. There are areas of the world where to be a realist is to catch, cook, and eat your neighbor. I looked objectively at the knife and dispassionately considered, nothing at all of the sharpness of the edge, but what would happen to the shape of the hand that held the knife. The evidence of what I might become in time was clear. I had only to look around the office in any direction to see it.

Actually, if you're in the land of the Hook Operators and if you graduate to the stage where you become a competitor for the same things the Hook Operators are after, your choices are few. You can become (1) another Hook Operator, (2) a bag of neuroses with a sack full of psychosomatic worry ailments, (3) a psychotic who escapes the conflict. There wasn't too much to choose from, but one fact stood out clearly. I didn't want a head full of hatchetman latticework. I went looking for another job and got it —down at the bottom of the ladder and good for another year or so, maybe longer, if I made sure I never became overly bright about learning the business.

The day I resigned I was a little blue. Would I ever get to be a really good practicing realist, I wondered. I decided, optimistically perhaps, that if I watched myself carefully, I never would.

# Appendix

*What follows is the full text of the set of definitions of Operators'
terms which Miss O'Brien transcribed at Hinton's direction and
took with her to the minister, the psychiatrist, and the psychoanalyst.*

*Operator.* A human being with a type of head formation which permits him to explore and influence the mentality of others.

*Thing.* A human being without the mental equipment of operators.

Board. Applied in layers to the minds of things. Serves as
protection.

*Shack.* Applied in shingles to the minds of things. Serves as a
protection.

*Stroboscope.* Equipment used to explore and influence the minds of
things. Can be used over a distance of one mile, in a straight line.

*Shoot temples full of shack.* A process which prevents the use of
stroboscope.

*Extend.* The ability of the operator to concentrate over distances.

*Latticework.* The structure of the mind of the thing which results
from habit patterns.

*Dummy.* A thing with very little latticework. Dummys are controlled
almost entirely by their operators.

*Sedation.* A mental stimulation of the operator which rests the thing.

*Dummetized.* A thing is dummetized when it has less latticework than
things usually have. Sometimes it is dummetized to permit greater
motivation by the operator, sometimes it is dummetized to allow
different habits to form.

*Block.* The concentration of the operator which blocks the mind of the thing and prevents its location or influence by other operators.

*Cordon.* Blocking the thing by a number of operators.

*Cover.* A device used by operators to work upon a thing's mind without disturbing other operators.

*Unravel.* To remove the cover.

*Aerate.* To expand the mentality and fill it with air.

*Expand.* To activate the mind of the thing so that it can function at top peak.

*Horse.* A term used by operators regarding things which can be worked the most easily. Sometimes called horse meat.

*Judicate.* To settle a contest between two operators. In the outcome of a draw, where the result is questioned by either of the operators involved, a judiciator is usually employed.

*Play, Double play.* Well thought out moves by operators to hook other operators.

*Hook.* Putting an operator in a position where he must move in some direction or pay off in points to get himself off the hook.

*Chisel.* To work on the temples of the thing to destroy its thinking powers. Extremely painful.

*Scallop.* To remove a thing's latticework. Less and less self-control is experienced by the thing.

*Rest.* To discontinue all operation by an operator on a thing.

*Prick seal.* Action taken by an operator to get through the seal placed over the mind of a thing to keep operators out.

200

*District.* The area under the jurisdiction of the operator employed as cop on beat.

*Shield.* An operator with authority to penalize other operators.

*Compounded expansion.* Applied in stripes to the mind of dummys to allow some self-control.

*Perfidy.* A penalty given to operators. The operator is unable to work while in perfidy. One and two days of perfidy are common sentences.

*Jeopardy.* Another penalty given to operators. Generally involves a jail sentence. Single jeopardy is a sentence of five days, double jeopardy, a sentence of ten days.

*Lien.* The operator having jurisdiction over the thing. Generally the lien is the employer or the closest relative of the thing.

*Chattel.* The operator having the permit to influence the thing while it is not under the influence of the lien. Generally, where the lien is an employer, the chattel is an operator situated close to the thing's home.

*Charter.* The operator having the thing's charter.

*Fly.* A term used for operators.

*Combine.* A group of operators which get together for some common purpose.

*Chipping Board.* A device used by operators to remove board from the head of a thing. If the board is new, it may be easily removed. This is referred to as devouring board.

*Close.* To close the mind so that other operators cannot enter easily to influence the thing.

*Open.* To open the mentality so that it can be influenced or observed easily.

*Shut.* To shut the mind of the thing so that operators cannot enter at all.

*Stone.* Mental concentration of one operator upon another operator. Stoned, an operator is wounded and cannot function. Stoning is accompanied by a great deal of head pain.

A certain percentage of the population has minds so constructed that they can influence the mentality of others and dominate them. These individuals are known as operators and refer to the rest of the population as things. Upon these things they establish liens, chattels, and charters and so retain options over them.

Primarily, an operator is concerned with making points. He does this usually by engaging in draws with other operators. In a draw, a group of operators are concerned with influencing the actions and thoughts of the thing. A selection of subjects is drawn up, one is chosen and each operator in turn enters and influences the thinking of the thing upon that subject. The operator who has had the greatest influence upon the thing and motivated its actions and thinking to the greatest extent wins the draw which means winning the points each operator has put up to enter the draw. When draws are questioned by operators, an authority given the authority judiciates it.

An operator can influence the mentality of people by extending his concentrating powers of from a distance of one half block to two blocks. Beyond that distance he must use stroboscope (equipment) to probe, feed in thoughts, take out information, or keep a watching eye on the person. A stroboscope is effective for a distance of one mile—in a straight line.

# Afterword

I carefully prepared a different afterword for *Operators and Things* and then I read the proof copy – twice. And as I was nearly the end, a strange thing happened.

As Barbara has offered some notes on Carl Jung, I don't feel shy adding that Jung wouldn't think that *any* happening was strange. In fact, a coincidence wouldn't be a coincidence but rather a meaningful series of events that were right to happen at precisely that moment. Ergo, at precisely the moment I finished the last page of the book I knew I needed to scrap my first draft and start over again.

Because what became perfectly clear—even though I've read this book a dozen times—was the tremendous insight these words have to offer. Again, this text provoked warm feelings, much akin to revisiting a dear friend from your past. And even though some of the information regarding mental health may be dated, the message it delivers is far from passé. Does insight ever go out of style?

As I sit at my computer, I'm hoping that I'm half as lucky as Barbara, and that the words that flow onto the page will tell a story as the story itself would like to be told.

In 1994, my writing partner, Melanie Villines, and I had just finished the first draft of our screenplay, *Operators and Things*. We were so jazzed about this project that our immediate reaction was, "Let's walk in Barbara's shoes," albeit nearly forty years later. Even though Melanie and I had separately experienced travel on a Greyhound bus, why not do it again? Why not take a few weeks off to experience life on the road, to travel willy-nilly through the country, hanging out in bus depots, eating at mom 'n pop diners, and sleeping in motels with flocked wallpaper?

As fun as it might have been, life didn't allow it. But instead, other interesting developments occurred. As we were doing our research, we filled one legal pad after another full of questions about Barbara. Curiosities were plentiful, answers were few. So what was Barbara really telling us? How could we retell this story?

Simply, we decided. We will stay true to the material.

So we set about carefully selecting the images and ideas that Barbara had meticulously constructed.

We felt that Sharp resembled Dionysius, the Greek god of grapes and the harvest. Additionally, Dionysius was the God of epiphany and the protector of those who do not belong to conventional society and much of which escapes human reasoning. To wit, many young people see the world as Sharp; life is full of hope and holds the promise of the future. But, as Barbara learned, it doesn't take long before reality sets in: jobs, responsibilities, duplicitous people, and hook operators. Voila! The bronco becomes the horse. Suddenly, Burt replaces Sharp and it's Burt's face in the mirror.

Curiously, Dionysius was also a friend of Pan, the god Nicky resembles, not only in his youthfulness but in his loyalty. Pan is associated with nature, sexuality, and spring. He also embodied, in his duality, the ability to incite panic (Pan) in crowded places as he passed through remote and lonely places. This is similar to what Barbara experienced as she fled Knox and set upon her journey throughout the country.

Also, consider this: there are three people – Burt, Sharp and Nicky – that Barbara first meets when she wakes up that morning. Three is a very symbolic number: it is the trinity in many religions; three is the ternary representing the spiritual and intellectual order, plus three wise men, three wishes, three blind mice. The list is endless.

It also didn't escape our notice that Barbara calls her sanity – or lack of – a dry beach. When she first goes to the psychiatrist, she can't think, can't remember, and can't communicate. She is virtually "dry." However, when she starts healing, the waves come, little by little, crashing over the dry beach, satiating her, restoring her soul and her mind. She starts to write, work, think and function. Symbolically, water is life. It is the river that carries us from birth until death. So when Barbara had no "water," she was insane. When water returned, so did her sanity.

These are only a few of the highlights this book has to offer. We are reissuing this classic in the hopes that Barbara's story will continue to fascinate and provoke thought in people the way it has for us. If this story liberates you, then it was no coincidence you happened to read it, now and just right now.

I'd like to think that's just what Barbara intended when she sat at the typewriter for the very first time.


COLLEEN DELEGAN

# A Conversation with
# Michael Maccoby, Ph.D.

### September 15, 2010

**It's been over a half-century since *Operators and Things* was published. How do you feel about the book after all this time?**

When you contacted me, I hadn't looked at the book for over fifty years. I reread it again before talking to you. And it holds up. It's a very compelling book.

**You were in your twenties when you wrote the introduction?**

I hadn't even gotten my doctorate yet.

**How did you get involved?**

I was then a graduate student at Harvard. I knew the publisher through the Signet Society at Harvard, which is a literary society where people have lunch together. He asked me whether I was interested in taking a look at this book. I said I'd think about it. I read it. I was very impressed by it. He asked me to write an introduction to it.

**You never met Barbara?**

No.

**When you read the book, did you ever have any doubts about its authenticity? Or did it have the ring of truth?**

For me, it had a ring of truth about it. Its critique of psychiatry and psychoanalysis was also very convincing.

**There are very few first-person accounts of schizophrenia. Why do you think that is?**

Few who have breakdowns have that kind of writing talent.

208

In the 1976 edition, Barbara wrote an update, where she discusses R.D. Laing in a section called "The New Minority." In his book *The Politics of Experience*, Laing references *Operators and Things* in very positive terms. He says, "For a beautifully lucid, autobiographical description of a psychotic episode that lasted six months, and whose healing function is clear, see Barbara O'Brien, *Operators and Things*."

The book had a big influence on him.

**Could you elaborate on that?**

Well in a book written by Daniel Burston – *The Wings of Madness: The Life and Work of R.D. Laing* – the author discusses how *Operators and Things* influenced Laing's idea about the positive functions of the visions and other symptoms in schizophrenia. Of course, in my introduction to *Operators and Things*, I wrote that.

**Yes you did.**

So R.D. Laing didn't mention the fact that he just took what I had written in the introduction and elaborated on it.

**Exactly. So that was plagiarism.**

As Picasso once said, "Small artists steal, great artists steal greatly."

**What is the main takeaway from the 1976 postscript?**

Barbara remained cured.

**In your introduction you mention that *Operators and Things* reads like a Hollywood script.**

Obviously, Barbara O'Brien is a very talented writer. Somebody who is a good writer will naturally put things in a way that are perhaps more dramatic. The characters, and the voices, and the people in the visions, these are not the illness; these are her attempts to cure herself. I found that that fit very well with some of Freud's writings.

**And in the introduction, you mention that Freud was influenced by Jung's observations**

I found that there was enough in Freud and Jung as well as a consistency in the book, the dynamics that it presented, that convinced me that it wasn't a made-up story.

**The book is masterful from a literary standpoint. I think the public appreciates it on that level, too.**

Yes, it's a good read.

**You hadn't read the book for fifty years, and you feel it still holds up.**

Yes. Right after I wrote the introduction, I got my doctorate and went to Mexico to work with Erich Fromm. I was out of the country for eight years. Maybe if I'd still been in the country, I would have gotten some comments at that time.

**As you look at the book now, what is the most striking thing?**

What stands out is her theory, where she attempted to understand how the physiological, particularly in the adrenal cortex, had some kind of relationship to her illness. She had to relearn how to fight, regain a sense of aggressiveness. You have to put that together with genetic vulnerability to schizophrenia, which we probably could learn more about now.

**Barbara had to become a bronco once again.**

She's extremely intelligent. That comes through in the book. This is an extremely intelligent individual.

**You say in your introduction, "Psychology does not know much about creativity." You also add, "creativity is a therapy by which Barbara transcends the psychiatrists' workaday world of confession and standardized inkblots." Well, you're an outstanding writer yourself, so you're able to recognize the quality of Barbara's writing as well as her creativity.**

At Harvard, I was president of the *Crimson*, the daily newspaper, so I did a lot of writing. I was in a class with people that included David Halberstam, John Updike, and a number of others who went on to become well-known writers. I had a very strong writing background. I've now published about thirteen books.

**You write that Barbara's playfulness and humor are her most impressive qualities. What is it about her humor that struck you?**

A sense of humor is the emotional equivalent of a sense of reality. If you don't have that sense of the absurd, you're out of reality. So she has a very powerful quality that connects her to reality. Play is one of our human drives that is the basis of creativity. All of the most creative people, whether they're artists or whether they're scientists, their work is really disciplined play. Play is what we do out of freedom, not necessity.

**You mentioned earlier that the book is fairly anti-psychiatry.**

Well, yes and no. It was antipsychiatry and rightly so, given the unfeeling way she was treated. Many psychiatrists are like that. And the psychoanalyst, that's a great dream she had about him being a third-rate racketeer. She does say the psychoanalyst is more understanding of her, but that he just had a stupid theory. There are psychotherapists who are sensitive. The fact is, I'm a psychoanalyst and I wrote the book's introduction.

# Biographies

BARBARA O'BRIEN is a pseudonym. *Operators and Things* was originally published in 1958, so the author was probably born in the late 1920s or early 1930s. In the 1976 paperback edition, her biography read: "Barbara O'Brien is now fully recovered and lives outside Los Angeles, California."

MICHAEL MACCOBY, Ph.D., is a psychoanalyst and anthropologist globally recognized as an expert on leadership for his research, writing, and projects to improve organizations and work. He has authored or co-authored twelve books and consulted to companies, governments, the World Bank, unions, research and development centers and laboratories, universities, and orphanages in twenty-six countries. He lives in Washington, DC.

COLLEEN DELEGAN's first life was an advertising creative director. Her second life is a screenwriter, novelist, and television writer. She is hoping for a third and final life as a wealthy nomad. She currently lives in Chicago.

MELANIE VILLINES is a critically acclaimed novelist, playwright, screenwriter, television writer, and biographer. Born and raised in Chicago, she lives in Los Angeles.

CPSIA information can be obtained at www.ICGtesting.com
Printed in the USA
LVOW10s2115300816

502505LV00031B/1328/P